An Introduction to Fernando Pessoa

Crosscurrents

An Introduction
to Fernando Pessoa

Modernism and the Paradoxcs of Authorship

Darlene J. Sadlier

University Press of Florida

Gainesville Tallahassee Tampa Boca Raton
Pensacola Orlando Miami Jacksonville

03 02 01 00 99 98 6 5 4 3 2 1

Library of Congress Cataloging-in-Publication Data

Sadlier, Darlene J. (Darlene Joy)
An introduction to Fernando Pessoa: modernism and the paradoxes
of authorship / Darlene J. Sadlier
p. cm.
Includes bibliographical references (p.) and index.
ISBN 0-8130-1583-9 (alk. paper)
1. Pessoa, Fernando, 1888–1935—Criticism and interpretation.
I. Title.
PQ9261.P417Z835   1998
869.1'41—DC21   97-35002

The University Press of Florida is the scholarly publishing agency for
the State University System of Florida, comprising Florida A & M
University, Florida Atlantic University, Florida International
University, Florida State University, University of Central Florida,
University of Florida, University of North Florida, University of
South Florida, and University of West Florida.

University Press of Florida
15 Northwest 15th Street
Gainesville, FL 32611
http://nersp.nerdc.ufl.edu/~upf

For Heitor Martins, scholar and friend,
and for Jim, who has made it all worthwhile.

Contents

Foreword

Issues of authorship, and its corollaries *origin*ality and *author*ity, have been at the heart of the modernist enterprise for the whole of our century. The breadth of authorial critique has ranged from James Joyce's exaltation (if not deification) of the author through his (admittedly egocentric) protagonist, Stephen Dedalus, in *A Portrait of the Artist as a Young Man,* ("The artist [is] like the God of creation") on the one hand, to the all-out assault on the hegemony of authorship launched by the Dadaists and Surrealists at about the same time through their collaborative productions, like the "exquisite corpse" experiments, and their advocacy of found art, like Marcel Duchamp's "ready-mades." The point is made strikingly by Max Ernst in the opening paragraph to his essay "Inspiration to Order": "Since the [making] of no work which can be called absolutely surrealist is to be directed consciously by the mind (whether through reason, taste, or the will), the active share of him hitherto described as the work's 'author' is suddenly abolished almost completely. This 'author' is disclosed as being a mere spectator of the birth of the work, for, either indifferently or in the greatest excitement, he merely watches it undergo the successive phases of its development." A generation later Roland Barthes would extend Ernst's polemic to conclude that "Surrealism . . . contributed to the desacralization of the image of the author. . . ."

With the diminution of the authorship passes the sacral quality of originality as well, a shift that may well have ushered in the age of pastiche, which on occasion we call postmodernism. Certainly, William Burroughs's and Brion Gysin's "cut-ups" are part of the devaluation of originality begun by, say, Tristan Tzara in his Dadaist phase. The central tropes for the death of "originality" may be Jorge Luis Borges's story "The Library of Babel" and his deconstruction of authorship in "Pierre Menard, Author of Don Quixote" (both available in *Ficciones* [New York: Grove Press, 1962]).

Between such extremes, the modernist writer has often taken a more ludic than sacral approach to the idea(l) of authorship. Marcel Proust created an alter ego named Marcel for his *roman fleuve, Remembrances of Things Past;* Samuel Beckett, a narrator named Sam for his narratological regression called *Watt.* The meticulous poet John Francis Shade was posthumously reconstituted by critic Charles Kinbote in Vladimir Nabokov's *Pale Fire.* Amid this company, but certainly less widely known and read than his international modernist contemporaries, is the Portuguese poet and critic Fernando Pessoa (1888–1935), but his explorations of the problematic of authorship admits him to the company of the century's major modernists. Darlene J. Sadlier's study, *An Introduction to Fernando Pessoa: Modernism and the Paradoxes of Authorship,* is one of the very few books in English on Pessoa, a writer who composed under nearly a hundred authorial guises he called not pseudonyms but "heteronyms," each with its distinct literary style. Like Yeats, Pessoa created "dialogue among imaginary voices." Like Joyce, Pessoa was often caught between "his nationalist versus his internationalist political inclinations." Like the hapless John Shade, Pessoa has been subject to reconfiguration by literary critics who "transformed him from a relatively unknown writer to a major poet of the Salazar regime. After the 1974 revolution, he was reconfigured yet again into a poet-symbol of the new democratic nation."

Sadlier focuses on four of the major "heteronyms," Alberto Caeiro, Ricardo Reis, Álvaro de Campos, and, of course, Fernando Pessoa, as she sets out to "demonstrate the complexity and versatility of his [their?] poetry, which ranges in style from an 'artless' simplicity to a subtle, almost Borgesian irony." Pessoa and the projections of his "artistic 'schizophrenia'" are finally "responsible for some of the most unusual and skillfully composed Portuguese verse in the twentieth century."

Such a study, then, not only enriches our understanding of international modernism, it constitutes an exemplary addition to the Crosscurrents series, which is designed to foreground comparative studies in European art and thought, particularly the intersections of literature and philosophy, aesthetics and culture. Without abandoning traditional comparative methodology, the series is also receptive to the latest currents in critical, comparative, and performative theory, especially that generated by the renewed intellectual energy in post-Marxist Europe. It will, as well, take full cognizance of the cultural and political realignments of what for the better part of the twentieth century have been two separated and isolated Europes. While, for instance, western Europe has, of late, been moving aggressively toward unification in the European Community, with the breakup of the twentieth century's last major colonial empire, the former Soviet Union, eastern Europe is retreating into nationalistic and religious enclaves with the collapse of the Communist hegemony. The intellectual, cultural, and literary significance of such profound restructuring, how history will finally rewrite itself, is difficult to anticipate. Having had a fertile period of modernism all but snuffed out in an ideological coup not long after the 1917 revolution, the nations of the former Soviet Union have, for the most part, been denied (or spared) the age of Freud and Jung, most modernist experiments, and postmodern fragmentation. Some Soviet writers have, of course, survived the putsch against modernism, in a literary underground that fed on *samizdat* publications; not the least of these is Andrei Bitov (b. May 27, 1937), whose *Pushkin House* (which was published in a *samizdat* version in Russia in 1971, in book form [in Russian] in the United States in 1978, and in book form in Russia not until 1989) established him as the heir to Nabokov and who may have helped Russian literature leap directly into postmodernism. And Bitov's current popularity in Russia and among the international literary community punctuates the return to experiment in Russian letters. But Bitov was a dim light in the darkness that was Soviet literary life. While western Europe continues reaching beyond modernism, eastern Europe may be struggling to recover its lost modernist heritage and so broaden its literary base. Whether a new art can emerge in the absence— or from the absence—of such forces as shaped European modernism is one of the intriguing questions of post–Cold War aesthetics, philosophy, and critical theory.

Darlene Sadlier's "Introduction" to Fernando Pessoa, then, helps broaden our understanding of European modernism and so forms precisely the sort of comparative philosophical and literary study that the Crosscurrents series was designed to foster. The series henceforth will continue to critique the developing, often conflicting currents of European thought through the prism of literature, philosophy, and theory.

S. E. Gontarski
Series Editor

Textual Note and Acknowledgments

As I show at a later point, there is considerable controversy surrounding the attempt to establish a "definitive" text for Fernando Pessoa. I have used various editions of his works, but my chief source is the Lello & Irmão edition *(Obra Poética e em Prosa)* published in 1986, which I chose because of its comprehensiveness, its notes and bibliography, and its compactness as a research tool. In all cases, I have provided my own English translations of Pessoa's writings; I try to offer fairly literal translations which the reader may compare with the original.

I was fortunate to receive grants from the Office for Research and the Graduate School and the West European Studies Program at Indiana University, Bloomington, to support the writing of this book. Portions of my book appeared in *diacrítica, Luso-Brazilian Review,* and the *Indiana Journal of Hispanic Literatures,* and I wish to thank Vítor Manuel de Aguiar e Silva for his early support of my work in this regard.

A number of individuals helped me with the research. In Lisbon, I am particularly grateful to Teresa Sobral Cunha, who guided me through the large archive of materials in the Biblioteca Nacional, and whose own work on Pessoa has been an inspiration; Manuela Nogueira, Pessoa's niece, who was most generous with her time and who, along with the Biblioteca Nacional, has graciously permitted me to quote from Pessoa's work in my book; and Maria Augusta de Figueiredo, who introduced me to Manuela and whose home has become my home whenever I'm in Portugal. Portuguese specialists David Jackson and Richard Zenith provided me with helpful comments on an early version of chapter 1. The Portuguese publisher Contexto has kindly granted me permission to use illustrations from their facsimile editions of *Portugal Futurista* and *Presença.* All other illustrations come from the Pessoa archive at the Biblioteca Nacional and are reproduced by permission. At Indiana, I want to thank my colleague Heitor Martins, who read parts of the manuscript; European specialists Hugo Kunoff and Nancy Boerner, who have built and maintained one of the finest libraries of Portuguese literature in the country; and James Naremore, who encouraged me to write this book, and who valiantly read and commented on the manuscript from beginning to end.

Introduction

On November 29, 1935, as he lay in a Lisbon hospital dying, Fernando Pessoa wrote, "I know not what tomorrow will bring." Whether one interprets this last line as a somber reflection on his health, as an expression of doubt, or simply as a banality, it is difficult to imagine that he could have foreseen what the future had in store for his reputation. When he died at the age of forty-seven, Pessoa was a relatively unknown Portuguese writer who had spent his life working as a commercial translator. Today, he is regarded as one of the major European poets of this century, and he has become a national icon in his Portuguese homeland. Without question, he was responsible for an intriguing poetic enterprise or verbal game that will keep editors and critics busy for decades to come.

Pessoa's name, in Portuguese, means "person," but one of his most interesting attributes was his habit of composing poems under different identities and in different styles. He created a gallery of authors, each with his own personal history, who also wrote essays on one another—including commentaries on Fernando Pessoa. In certain ways, these various characters, which he called "heteronyms," are symptomatic of modernist literary technique in general; they have something in common with Yeats's "masks" and Pound's "personae," and are a logical outgrowth of modernism's attempt to make poetry seem impersonal or purely dramatic. But Pessoa also makes us aware of the more general crisis of subjectivity in nineteenth- and twentieth-century philosophy. Like Kierkegaard, he invents different authorial personalities who embody contrasting views of life; like Nietzsche, he suggests that the self is "something that must be created"; and like Foucault, he seems to believe that "one writes to become someone other than who one is."

Actually, Pessoa was not one author but many, each of whom deserves a place in modern literary history. In different poetic guises, he was lover and ascetic, revolutionary and conservative, futurist and classicist. All of his intellectual, political, and artistic interests were contradictory. As a student of astrology and theosophy, he seems to have believed in clairvoyance and mystical experience; he even created elaborate horoscopes to chart the future for himself and his major identities: Alberto Caeiro, Ricardo Reis, and Álvaro de Campos. At the same time, he was a skeptic who implicitly questioned the ability to know anything outside language itself. A flaneur, a voyeur, and a literary dandy, Pessoa stood aside from the historical events of his day and lived in relative obscurity; but he was also a strong ego who believed that his career was linked to the future of the Portuguese nation. One of his most spirited essays predicts a cultural revolution to be ushered in by a "Supra-Camões," or a poet like "himself," who would somehow transcend Portugal's most celebrated Renaissance author.

This book is designed to explore some of the cultural, political, and personal tensions that led to Pessoa's artistic "schizophrenia." My aim is to demonstrate the complexity and versatility of his poetry, which ranges in style from an "artless" simplicity to a subtle, almost Borgesian irony; but I also want to show how the four major heteronyms ("Pessoa" included) are related to one another. I am certainly not the first writer who has attempted to find a structural connection between the heteronyms, although I have explained this connection in slightly different ways from previous critics.[1] Whatever their relationship, the four "authors" are responsible for some of the most unusual and skillfully composed Portuguese verse in the twentieth century. My overriding purpose is to introduce them to a broad readership in the English-speaking world while offering a commentary on their writings that will also interest the specialist in Portuguese literature. In most cases, I have avoided close readings of the major poems, preferring instead to concentrate on larger issues of style, ideology, psychology, and cultural politics. For similar reasons, I have not attempted to describe or synthesize the vast body of interpretive criticism on individual verses. I cite many scholarly essays, and I provide a selective but fairly extensive bibliography. In general, however, my purpose is to combine an overview of the major heteronyms with a detailed analysis of the origins and cultural implications of Pessoa's enterprise as a whole.

There are too few English-language studies on Pessoa, a situation that is unfortunate not only because of the great importance of his poetry but also because he wrote in English on many occasions. Born in Lisbon in 1888 and raised in South Africa, Pessoa was educated in British schools, where he excelled in composition, literature, and translation of the classics. He admired Shakespeare and Milton, he adored *Pickwick Papers,* and much of his mature poetry bears the imprint of his schoolboy fascination with the

British romantics and Edgar Allan Poe. Even after he returned to Portugal in 1905, he remained aware of contemporary developments in the poetry of both Britain and the United States. At this time, he was composing dreamy verses under the guise of "Alexander Search," whose poems about a "thinking and feeling" self anticipate a dialectical tension that we can find in many of the later heteronyms. He also wrote long commentaries in English about literary history, theory, and aesthetics. In later years, he wrote prefaces to introduce Portuguese literary movements and authors (including the authors he had created), offering them to a prospective English editor. He probably was seeking a career as an international poet; indeed, with the exception of his modernist "epic," *Mensagem [Message]*, which appeared just prior to his death, the only books he published during his life comprised his English verses.[2] Ironically, these slim volumes, which were printed in Portugal, were relatively conventional and had virtually no readership. Pessoa's reputation as a major poet derives instead from his writings in Portugal's literary periodicals, where he synthesized international modernism with distinctly Portuguese traditions.

Notwithstanding his love of English, Pessoa immersed himself in his native language and literature. Among his favorite authors were the romantics, especially Almeida Garrett, and the late-nineteenth-century poets Antero de Quental, António Nobre, Camilo Pessanha, and Cesário Verde. After the proclamation of the First Portuguese Republic in 1910, he began publishing newspaper articles about Portuguese literature, and he instigated some lively literary debates. He enjoyed the *sucess du scandale* of *Orpheu* (1915), a vanguard literary review to which he contributed drama and poetry under his own name. Álvaro de Campos, a somewhat Whitmanesque and futurist heteronym, made his first appearance in the pages of this journal, although the "pagan" Alberto Caeiro and the "neo-classic" Ricardo Reis (who already existed) had to wait another decade to make their public debut.

In fact, although Pessoa published in a variety of literary forums over the years, his published works constitute only a fraction of what he actually wrote. His archive in the Biblioteca Nacional is an amazing collection of thousands of manuscripts of every genre which he had tucked away in his apartment. Despite his considerable talents as a prose writer (among his most notable works is the "diary" entitled *Livro do Desassossego [The Book of Disquiet]* by "Bernando Soares," his preferred genre was poetry. His heteronymous verses are clearly his greatest achievement, and it is this aspect of his writing that my book explores in detail.

My study places the Portuguese lyric and epic poems in their historical context, giving attention to some of the political events that helped shape Portuguese literature in general and Pessoa's writing in particular. Pessoa lived during a turbulent period, witnessing the demise of a centuries-old monarchy, the birth and death of a republic, and the installation of a right-wing military dictatorship. With each new change in government, he hoped for the transformation of his poor, agrarian homeland into a cosmopolitan and powerful nation, not unlike the "Fifth Empire," which he wrote about in *Mensagem*. His writings over the years—especially his essays—are an important record of this period, and they reflect his moments of great optimism as well as his skepticism about Portugal's political and literary future.

Pessoa's different personae may have grown out of his simultaneous attraction to a traditional style, rooted in Portuguese medieval and Renaissance lyrics, and to a modern aesthetic derived from French symbolism. But the various poets he created cannot be explained by any single motive. As my first chapter demonstrates, Pessoa was disposed from his childhood onward to a kind of literary ventriloquism; his aesthetic depended on techniques of pastiche or quotation, which ultimately formed into dramatic characters or full-fledged authors. These authors served various functions, indicating a number of possible "splits" in his subjectivity: they allowed him to explore the "romantic" versus "classic" tendencies within modernism; they enabled him to express his nationalist versus his internationalist political inclinations; and, on a more psychological level, they offered him the chance to participate in a kind of masquerade in which he sometimes could experience emotions he did not allow "himself" to feel.

The different "faces" of Pessoa tended to multiply and develop splits within themselves. By the same token, the different authors sometimes overlapped with one another. In my individual chapters on Pessoa, Caeiro, Reis, and Campos, I try to describe the stylistic and thematic characteristics of the four major poets, but I also point out certain overlooked affinities among them, challenging the generally held notion that they have solid identities. To complicate matters still further, my study concludes with a discussion of various images of Pessoa that have been created by scholars and critics after his death. In my final chapter, I am especially interested in the posthumous editing of his work, which transformed him from a relatively unknown writer to a major poet of the Salazar regime. After the 1974 revolution, he was reconfigured yet again into a poet-symbol of the new democratic nation. The irony of this process is that each change in Pessoa's identity has involved an attempt to fix an image for a writer who was, by the very nature of his career, a protean figure. Pessoa always questioned the idea of a stable identity, whereas criticism has tended to construct him as a solid personality with clear intentions.

Pessoa's instability as an author is a vexing problem for anyone who tries to analyze him, and the organization of my book may suggest a logic and coherence that his work does not truly have. The ever-changing, chameleonlike quality of his writing is described in a "personal note" that he composed in English in 1910: "I am now in full possession of the fundamental laws of literary art. Shakespeare can no longer teach me to be subtle, nor Milton to be complete. My intellect has attained a pliancy and a reach that enable me to assume any emotion I desire and enter at will into any state of mind" (2:86).[3]

Because of his technical skill, he had an ability to move back and forth "at will" between "Pessoa" and the other heteronyms, composing radically different kinds of texts within the space of a single day. Unfortunately, the polyphonic or dramatic aspect of his poetry has been lost in the anthologies and editions that appeared after his death. Instead of publishing his work in chronological sequence, the editors separated the writings by Pessoa "himself" from those of the major heteronyms, giving each "author" different volumes. In making this decision, scholars were guided by certain organizational notions that Pessoa mentioned in letters to friends, but a close examination of the letters reveals that he constantly changed his mind about how his work should be arranged. In 1915, for example, Pessoa wrote to his friend Armando Cortes-Rodrigues that he was ready to launch "pseudonymously" the work of Caeiro-Reis-Campos.[4] Seventeen years later, writing to the critic João Gaspar Simões, he was still anticipating this project and debating with himself about its proper organization:

> Primitivamente, era minha intenção começar as minhas publicações por três livros, na ordem seguinte: (1) *Portugal,* que é um livro pequeno de poemas (tem 41 ao todo), de que o *Mar Português (Contemporânea 4)* é a segunda parte; (2) *Livro do Desassossego* (Bernardo Soares, mas subsidiariamente, pois que o B.S. não é um heterónimo, mas uma personalidade literária); (3) *Poemas Completos de Alberto Caeiro* (com o prefácio de Ricardo Reis, e, em posfácio, as *Notas para a Recordação* do Álvaro de Campos). Mais tarde, no outro ano, seguiria, só ou com qualquer livro, *Cancioneiro* (ou outro título igualmente inexpressivo), onde reuniria (em *Livros I a III*

ou *I a V*) vários dos muitos poemas soltos que tenho, e que são por natureza inclassificáveis salvo de essa maneira inexpressiva. (2:307–8)

[Early on it was my intention to begin my publications with three books in the following order: (1) *Portugal,* which is a small book of poems (41 in all), of which *Portuguese Sea (Contemporânea 4)* is the second part; (2) *The Book of Disquiet* (Bernardo Soares, but subsidiarally, since B.S. is not a heteronym but a literary personality); (3) *The Complete Poems of Alberto Caeiro* (with a preface by Ricardo Reis and, as an afterword, the *Notes for a Remembrance* by Álvaro de Campos). Later, the next year would follow, alone or with some other book, *Cancioneiro* (or another equally unexpressive title), where I would bring together (in *Books I to III* or *I to V*) several of the many loose poems that I have and which are unclassifiable by nature, except in this unexpressive form.]

Immediately following this passage, Pessoa listed several doubts and financial concerns—as if he were unable or reluctant to carry out his plan. Then only a few paragraphs later, he suggested publishing the poems of the heteronyms under his own name, in a series entitled *Ficções do Interlúdio* [Fictions of the interlude]. The series would include a volume of aesthetic debates by Pessoa "himself," Ricardo Reis, Álvaro de Campos, and perhaps one or two other heteronyms. Referring to the heteronyms, Pessoa writes, "ainda há um ou outro (incluindo um astrólogo) para aparecer" [there's still one or more (including an astrologer) to appear] (2:309).

Although tentative in his outline of a series, Pessoa proposed in his letter to Simões that the first volume (on Caeiro) should contain, in addition to the afterword by Campos: "3 ou 5 *livros* das *Odes* do Ricardo Reis. O volume, assim, conterá o essencial para se compreender o início da 'escola': as obras do Mestre e algumas do discípulo directo, incluindo (nas *Notas*) alguma coisa já do outro discípulo" [3 or 5 *books* of the *Odes* by Ricardo Reis. Thus, the volume will contain all that's essential for understanding the beginning of the "school": the works of the Master and some by his direct disciple, including (in the *Notes*) something already by the other disciple] (2:309). The design here is interesting to contemplate because it arranges the poetry in scholarly or historical form, almost like an imaginary Borgesian library, reflecting the linear development of a nonexistent school of literature.[5] In typical fashion, however, Pessoa ended his letter by undercutting the proposal: "Tudo isto, porém, é incerto" [All of this, however, is uncertain] (2:309).

Despite the lack of any definitive plan, Pessoa's projected volume on the "beginning of the school" and his idea for a book of aesthetic debates by his various personae would have embodied one of his more distinctive traits often noted by critics—that is, his habit of creating a dialogue among imaginary voices. I would argue that this particular form of intertextuality can be fully appreciated only through a chronological or historical reading of his texts. Although my own chapters have tended to follow the structure that editors have given posthumously to Pessoa's works, I have tried throughout to emphasize the central importance of the dramatic interaction among the poets.

In this context, I should also note that although Pessoa had a propensity for founding "schools," none of his poetic identities assumes an importance greater than the others. Thus, while I begin my survey of the four major authors with the poetry of Pessoa "himself," I do not want to suggest that his writings under his own name are privileged. Pessoa repeatedly acknowledged Caeiro as the *Mestre* [Master] of the group; but he also deferred to Campos, whose dramatic, bombastic, and sometimes painfully introspective lyrics are regarded by many critics as the most compelling of Pessoa's writings. Pessoa regularly referred to "himself" in the third person—perhaps because, like the heteronyms, the writings signed under his name represented a dramatic personality rather than a historical subject. Nowhere does he state this fact more clearly than in a fragment he wrote on being Portuguese: "O bom português é várias pessoas . . . Nunca me sinto tão portuguesmente eu como quando me sinto diferente de mim—Alberto Caeiro, Ricardo Reis, Álvaro de Campos, Fernando Pessoa, e quantos mais haja havidos ou por haver." [The good Portuguese is various persons . . . Never do I feel so Portuguese as when I feel that I am different from me— Alberto Caeiro, Ricardo Reis, Álvaro de Campos, Fernando Pessoa, and as many more as have been or will be] (2:1014).

Of course at some level, what is true of the "good Portuguese" is equally true of all writers. If this were not the case, Pessoa would not have emerged as one of the most fascinating poets of the twentieth century. Thus, alongside my attempt to make Pessoa coherent, I also want to make the reader aware that I am dealing with a writer who tends to deconstruct his various personalities, casting doubt on the idea of individual authorship. My own attitude toward this phenomenon is strongly influenced by such theorists as Michel Foucault and Roland Barthes, whose writings I cite at several junctures. I agree with Foucault, for example, when he says that the "author function" is closely tied to the discursive institutions of literature, and to the critical need to *classify* texts, thereby establishing a "relationship of

homogeneity, filiation, authentification of some texts by the use of others."
At bottom, such relationships are always "projections," governed by the
belief that there must be "a point where contradictions are resolved, where
incompatible elements are at last tied together or organized around a fundamental originating contradiction."[6] In the history of Pessoa scholarship,
we can see exactly this sort of intellectual rage for order. Shortly after
Pessoa died in 1935, more than twenty-five thousand of his unpublished
items were discovered in a trunk in his apartment, and it is chiefly from
these manuscripts, along with many others discovered subsequently, that
his reputation and his personae have been built. "How shall we recognize
a work among the many traces left by a man after his death?" Foucault has
asked rhetorically, and Pessoa's editors set out precisely to answer that
question. My final chapter speculates on their work, showing how they
gradually transformed what Foucault and Barthes would call a "text" into
a more stable and commodified series of "works" by a great author.

Having said this, let me quickly add that I do not believe Pessoa's editors
or any subsequent critics were making an error. Nor do I believe that Pessoa
can be read in any way one wishes. My point is simply that Pessoa's evolv-
ing identities need to be placed in a cultural context, and that we need to
pay some attention to the shifting critical reception of his verse. I am certainly not writing a book about the "death of the author." (Even Foucault
and Barthes were not making that claim, although readers sometimes re-
duce their arguments to a vulgar deconstruction.) On the contrary, I am
trying to show that Pessoa was a creative individual who desired fame and
who posthumously achieved many of his authorial ambitions. At the same
time, I want to show that he was one of those peculiarly modern writers
who, either intentionally or inadvertently, seemed to "loosen" what
Barthes has called "the sway of the Author."[7] Like Mallarmé, Proust,
Joyce, and many other key figures of modernism and postmodernism,
Pessoa's authority is achieved paradoxically by a subordination of romantic authorship to a kind of ever-changing mimicry or textual performance.
Throughout my study, I have attempted to demonstrate this fact, which
may suggest a good deal about the nature of literature in general.

1

Pessoa's Juvenilia and the Origins
of "Heteronymous" Poetry

Pessoa composed an impressive array of materials as a youth, some of which date back as far as 1902, when he and his family had temporarily returned to Lisbon from Durban, South Africa, where his stepfather was the Portuguese consul. Among these items—many in fragmentary form—are poems, stories, essays, word games, and long lists of titles for prospective works to be penned by various fictional personalities. Several poems and prose fragments from the period 1902 to 1907 appear in editions of Pessoa's collected works published after his death in 1935, and other aspects of his writing in this period are documented by Alexandrino Severino and H. D. Jennings, who wrote important studies of Pessoa's childhood years in South Africa. More recently, Teresa Rita Lopes has edited a volume of largely unpublished materials that includes facsimiles of many early manuscripts. This valuable edition emphasizes the scope of his literary activity as well as his exceptional talent. As yet, however, Pessoa's earliest writings have received no extended critical or theoretical analysis.[1] They deserve much closer attention because Pessoa was unquestionably a prodigy, and his adolescent work is conceptually and stylistically far more sophisticated than what we normally describe as juvenilia.

As the following chapter will show, the verse and linguistic games of Pessoa's youth have important implications for the artistic strategies and cultural politics that would animate his entire career as a writer. These implications are especially evident in two ostensibly different examples of his writings from 1902: a short poem representing his official public debut and a series of handwritten, unpublished "newspapers" whimsically entitled O Palrador [The chatterer] and A Palavra [The word]. Both the poem and the newspapers reveal that from the age of fourteen Pessoa was intrigued by devices such as imitation, quotation, and parody and that he aimed to construct a kind of literary dialogue with other authors, some of whom he created as personae or imaginary aspects of himself. Here and in his later work, his aesthetic always involved forms of visible impersonation, explicit appropriation, and overt intertextuality—principles ultimately refined into one of the most unusual projects of European modernism, which he described as "heteronymous" poetry.

Of course all writing is intertextual, because it depends on an interpretive community's awareness of convention and precedent, or on what Jonathan Culler has described as a "general discursive space" through which messages are understood. Even so, we can make distinctions among different authors according to the way they use prior materials. Some writers emphasize their own originality, leaving us to debate about the possible sources of their works; others are quite specific and open about the process of borrowing, and their art depends on a perceptible relation between a "new" text and some kind of tradition. Then, too, writers can be more or less eclectic in their selections of sources. Every writer who quotes or imitates an earlier text helps to establish a potential canon, and we can classify different authors according to the degree to which they borrow from "high" or "low" models, from ancients or contemporaries, from established masters or from obscure talents.[2] In what follows, I shall argue that Pessoa was in some ways a classicist or strong conservative who engaged in imitation of an elite literary tradition. But his techniques were also distinctly modern; he blurs the boundaries between influence, imitation, and forgery, and he requires his readers to rethink the nature of authorship. These contradictory aspects of his verse will become more clear if we examine representative examples of his early writing in detail.

Old Becomes New: The "Mote e Glosa"

Pessoa's first known published poem appeared in the July 18, 1902, issue of the Portuguese newspaper *O Imparcial* during a period when he and his family were residing in Lisbon. A brief prefatory note introduces the author as "uma simpática e irrequieta criança de 14 anos, de espírito vivo e inteligente" [an engaging and restless 14-year-old, with a lively and intelligent spirit]. The poem reads as follows:

Mote
Teus olhos, contas escuras,
São duas Ave Marias
D'um rosário d'amarguras
Que eu rezo todos os dias.

Glosa
Quando a dor me amargurar,
Quando sentir penas duras,

Só me podem consolar
Teus olhos, contas escuras.

Deles só brotam amores,
Não há sombras d'ironias
Esses olhos sedutores
São duas Ave Marias.

Mas se a ira os vem turvar
Fazem-me sofrer torturas
E as contas todas rezar
D'um rosário d'amarguras.

Ou se os alaga a aflição
Peço p'ra ti alegrias
N'uma fervente oração
Que rezo todos os dias![3]

[Motif
Your eyes, dark beads,
Are two Ave Marias
In a rosary of sorrows
That I pray every day.

Gloss
When suffering embitters me,
When I feel sharp pains,
Only your eyes, dark beads,
Can console me.

From them love alone bursts forth,
With no shades of irony.
Those seductive eyes
Are two Ave Marias.

But if anger should cloud them over
Then I suffer tortures
And I pray with all the beads
In a rosary of sorrows.

Or if grief wells up in them
I ask happiness for you
In a fervent prayer
That I pray every day!]

These apparently simple lines contain a relatively complex series of allusions or historical associations, demonstrating Pessoa's learning and precocity. The verse form, for instance, is a "mote e glosa" [motif and gloss], the earliest written examples of which appear in Garcia de Resende's compilation of fifteenth- and early-sixteenth-century Portuguese palace poetry, the *Cancioneiro Geral* (1516). The "mote e glosa" composition—also known as "poesia obrigada a mote" [poetry bound to the motif]—can be dated back to the Middle Ages and was frequently performed in the court, where a poet could showcase his skill by constructing *glosas* that emulated another poet's verse. One of the rules of the form was that the earlier poet should be directly quoted in the beginning of the text and identified as the "mote alheio" [foreign motif], or simply the *mote*.[4]

Interestingly, however, the lines selected by Pessoa for his *mote* are not from a late-medieval or early-Renaissance source but from Augusto Gil's "Cantigas," in the volume entitled *Versos,* first published in 1901.[5] The citation of Gil gives a further historical dimension to the poem, calling attention to the fact that Pessoa's contemporaries and immediate predecessors throughout Europe—including the pre-Raphaelites, the symbolists, and the *fin-de-siècle* decadents—often used imagery or verse forms that vaguely suggested the Middle Ages. (See also the early work of the modernist generation in England, especially Yeats and Pound.) Pessoa's "mote e glosa" therefore suggests a witty faux-medievalism, in the sense that he employed variations on a *mote* he had taken from a contemporary text that was *already* alluding to the themes of troubadour love poetry. At the same time, Pessoa was much more "authentic" than Gil in the way he used an older form. Adopting a precise recipe from courtly poetry, he wrote four stanzas (a total that corresponds to the number of lines in the *mote*), and he used the seven-syllable *redondilha* as well as rhyme in his elaboration of the motif. In this last respect, he highlighted still another poetic reference or echo that should be noted: while the image of the woman's eyes and the themes of sorrow and consolation in the *mote* are reminiscent of both troubadour love poetry and late romanticism, they also call to mind the lyric verse of Portugal's major Renaissance poet, Luís Vaz de Camões, many of whose best known poems are *redondilhas* in the form of *glosas* on the power of a woman's eyes to save or destroy.[6]

Given the fame of Camões as a master of the *redondilha*, it is tempting to employ Harold Bloom's ideas about literary influence, arguing that Camões, not Gil or the palace poets, was the "father figure" and the rival Pessoa sought to emulate. Indeed, a decade after the appearance of his "mote e glosa," Pessoa predicted that a new literary master, or "Supra-

Camões," was imminent—a figure who would relegate the "Great Poet" to a secondary status (2:1153). But the relationship between Pessoa and his many sources is rarely conflicted or repressed, and it cannot be explained adequately in terms of Oedipal anxiety over a strong precursor. In his "mote e glosa," Pessoa was faithful to the example of late-medieval and early-Renaissance practitioners, who proved their expertise by constructing new poems out of old ones; his novelty lay in the fact that his verse was more historically playful, drawing on models from both the immediate and the distant past. A true modernist, he differed from a writer like Gil in that he cultivated an art of recontextualization and open quotation rather than an art of romantic expressiveness.

The "debut" poem shows that from the beginning Pessoa was an especially self-reflexive and erudite writer who invited his readers to consider how specific works relate to tradition or context. All of his subsequent poetry functioned along these lines, and was therefore intensely literary, drawing on his knowledge of periods as distinct as Ancient Greece, Elizabethan England, and Republican Portugal. He frequently expressed his admiration for Shakespeare, the British romantics, Whitman, and nineteenth-century Portuguese poets. He regularly borrowed from these and other sources, and, in a more radical move, he eventually demonstrated a strong inclination toward a kind of masquerade and artistic "forgery."[7] Throughout his career, his work depended on visible citation or appropriation, as if he wanted to problematize romantic ideas of originality.

Of course Pessoa did not simply revert to earlier models. As Peter Rickard states in the introduction to his English translation of Pessoa's mature verse: "From time to time we may hear an echo or sense an affinity, but it is as though the Portuguese poet, so far as he used other people's ideas or images, deliberately used them in new and startling ways."[8] Skills of this kind, typical of the early practitioners of the "mote e glosa," could be appreciated only by an educated and sensitive audience, who could recognize the play of densely intertextual verse. Pessoa implied as much when he wrote that he later created a coterie of fictional poets or "heteronyms" in order to assuage his need for an elite interpretive community: "Com uma tal falta de gente coexistível, como há hoje, que pode um homem de sensibilidade fazer senão inventar os seus amigos, ou, quando menos, os seus companheiros de espírito?" [With such a lack of compatible people, as is the case today, what can a man of sensibility do but invent his friends, or, at the very least, his spiritual companions?] (2:1022).

Unlike the court poet, who participated in a ludic contest with other versifiers, the mature Pessoa ultimately developed his own supporting network of critical and poetic discourse: he composed complete bodies of poetry under the guise of imaginary personalities, each with his own style and elaborately constructed history. There were an indeterminate number of these writers, but the principal work was "authored" by Alberto Caeiro, Ricardo Reis, Álvaro de Campos, and Pessoa "himself."[9] As the subsequent chapters of this book will demonstrate, the four major heteronyms are to some extent imitations of already recognizable poetic styles or schools. Three of the four also serve as critics, explicating and expounding on the work of the others. Imbued with a vast cultural memory, they weave together the sum total of Pessoa's own cultural expertise, formed from his extensive readings in Portuguese, English, and other national literatures.[10]

Pessoa's first published poem is a small but important indicator of the tendency toward imitation that led him to his rich collection of heteronymous poetry. In later years, in a note written in English bearing the title "The Uselessness of Criticism," he expressed his skepticism about the critic's ability to perceive the special kind of originality or "constructiveness" in his method. His remarks function rather like a theoretical defense of the techniques we have seen in the "mote e glosa":

> Let us suppose a deeply original work of art comes before [the critic's] eyes. How does he judge it? By comparison with the works of art of the past. If it be original, however, it will depart in something—and the more original the more it will depart—from the works of art of the past . . . And if its originality, instead of lying in a departure from those old standards, lie in a use of them on more severely constructive lines—as Milton used the ancients—will the critic take that bettering to be a bettering, or the use of those standards to be an imitation? Will he rather see the builder than the user of the building materials? Why should he rather do one thing than the better one? Of all elements, constructiveness is the most difficult to determine in a work . . . A fusion of past elements: will the critic see the fusion of the elements? (3:124)[11]

One Becomes Many: The Newspapers

Other aspects of Pessoa's "constructiveness" are evident in O Palrador and A Palavra, two "newspapers" he created during several months in 1902.[12] Handwritten, elaborately designed, and totally fictional, these newspapers are parodies or pastiches of literary journalism. They survive in the form of meticulously detailed manuscripts containing an array of news items, poems, word games, and drawings, and they are fascinating to contemplate

A facsimile of the front page of O *Palrador* (1902), one of Pessoa's handwritten "newspapers."

both as art objects and as "forgeries." They employ the same kinds of allusion or quotation as we have seen in the "mote e glosa," but they add an important new effect: like Pessoa's later poetry, they are filled with nonexistent authors who engage in dialogue with historical tradition.

If Pessoa's choice of the "mote e glosa" for one of his earlier poems suggests a certain nostalgia for the hierarchy of the Portuguese court, his interest in the newspaper seems to point in a distinctly modern direction. It is doubtful, however, that he was attracted to journalism for democratic reasons. Pessoa grew up in a culture in which newspapers gave poets direct access to a literate audience. In fact, his fictional imitations resemble eighteenth-century coffee-house journals more than modern, mass-circulation dailies. At the same time, he seems to have been intrigued with the way the journalistic medium involved several voices at play with one another in the columns of a single page. In the case of the early "mote e glosa," Pessoa had emulated another author and created a new work whose most notable feature is, to borrow a phrase from Julia Kristeva, its "mosaic of quotations."[13] In the case of the newspapers, he mimicked various kinds of writing, including poetry, prose, and word games; more importantly, he also began to compose under the guise of different personalities—each of whom is given a literary style, an area of expertise, and, in many cases, a name.

In a now-famous letter to the Portuguese critic Adolfo Casais Monteiro, in which he describes the genesis of his heteronyms, Pessoa remarked that during his childhood he enjoyed inventing fictional writers. The letter mentions in particular the "Chevalier de Pas," whom Pessoa describes as his first heteronym or "conhecido inexistente" [nonexistent acquaintance]—an imaginary persona who composed letters to Pessoa when he was six years old (2:340). The childhood letters do not survive, but the various personae in *O Palrador* and *A Palavra* are similar to the Chevalier de Pas and are among the first important manifestations of Pessoa's desire to create an imaginary literary community. Significantly, after his return to South Africa in 1902, Pessoa continued writing under a variety of names in Portuguese as well as English and French. Among the signatures that appear in the miscellany of largely fragmentary materials from this period are "Alexander Search," "C. R. Anon," "Dr. Pancrácio," and "Jean Seul." He even had a calling card embossed with the name of Alexander Search, and one of his manuscripts bears the stamp of a seal engraved "C. R. Anon"— one of his most flamboyant youthful creations, who engaged in an amusing poetic polemic in the pages of the Durban newspaper, *The Natal Mercury*.[14]

The three issues of *O Palrador,* the more elaborate of Pessoa's fictional newspapers, are dated March 22 (no. 5), May 24 (no. 6), and July 5 (no. 7). (Three years later, when Pessoa once again found himself in Lisbon, he revived this paper with a single issue, dated September 17, 1905.) The only issue of *A Palavra* is dated May 15, 1902, although a supplement to an issue dated May 16 also survives. In the construction of *O Palrador,* Pessoa not only drew up a column format but also provided an intricate masthead which includes, in addition to the date, number, issue, price, and address of the newspaper, the names of the editorial and administrative staff. There

Pessoa's experiments with signatures for Alexander Search.

are other interesting graphic touches: Pessoa frequently employed bolder and varied lettering in an attempt to represent fonts for headlines and other important materials; and in a few places, he seems to have intentionally varied the written signatures of his different authors, as if to provide further proof of their reality.[15]

The items in both newspapers tend to be fanciful and amusing. For example, the lead article in issue six of O Palrador is a long piece entitled "Monstros da Antiguidade" [Monsters from antiquity], authored by a "Fr. Angard." Listed as part of the series "Leituras Científicas" [Scientific readings], the article is a cleverly written, encyclopedic account of the fantastic creatures that populated land and sea during the dinosaur age. A second lengthy article, entitled "A Pesca das Pérolas" [Fishing for pearls], written by a "Dr. Calviro," follows the dinosaur piece and is subtitled "Mais a Sério" [More in the serious vein].[16] This article, like the first, captures the enthusiasm of the youthful Pessoa for the fantastic world of the sea and perhaps also for what he later described as his "inborn tendency to mystification, to artistic lying" (2:73). Other categories of prose range from "serious" journalism and daily news items to comic dialogues, fictional sketches, and gossipy anecdotes. Each of these genres is treated in gently ironic fashion. For example, the May 15 issue of A Palavra contains a brief tale about an astrologer who, having correctly predicted the death of the king's beloved, is about to be executed for having brought tragedy into the king's life. Before the king can give the signal for the execution, the astrologer makes one final prediction: that his death will precede by three days the king's own demise. The short piece ends on an ironic note as the king decides to forgo giving the signal.

One of the entries in the May 15 issue of A Palavra is signed by a "Dr. Pancrácio," although the masthead identifies Fernando Pessoa as the director and M. N. Freitas, Pessoa's Azorean cousin, as the editor. On the masthead of the supplementary issue, Dr. Pancrácio is placed in parentheses beside Pessoa's name, as if to suggest a kind of mask rather than a complete character. In most ways, however, *A Palavra* is truly newspaperlike, because it assimilates the various "contributors" into a single, heterogeneous, yet somehow unified text, comprising different generic categories. By contrast, *O Palrador* is overtly literary and is filled with bylines. A chronological examination of the three surviving issues reveals a steady decrease in the number and length of prose entries and a corresponding increase in the number of poems, some of which take the form of "charades." Although nowadays we associate charades with a parlor game in which individuals pantomime words and phrases, the term has a larger meaning derived from the Provençal *charrado* [chatter], and it initially signified a written riddle. Like the "mote e glosa," the particular form of this riddle is based on a challenge that requires players to recontextualize a specific word, phrase, or stanza. In issue seven of *O Palrador,* for example, the author known as "Pip" addresses his charade to "Parry," while "Gee" and the couple "Morris and Theodor" challenge Pip to decipher a "metagram" and a "logogriph." In fact, each newspaper lists the names and scores of all those "participants" who responded to the previous issue's charades. The lists contain the names of numerous individuals who appear only in this section, among them, "Zé Nabos" [Joe Turnips], "Rabanete" [Radish], and "Trapalhão" [Blunderer].[17] The paper also recognizes the accomplishments of certain players whose charades had stumped the readers of previous issues.

The variety of fictional poets in the newspaper is remarkable, ranging from light versifiers to fully embodied romantic authors. At one extreme is Pip, whose name probably derives from Pessoa's boyhood admiration for Dickens. The poem by this author, entitled "Os Ratos," is written in the traditional *redondilha* style and is a charming, albeit somewhat morbid, nursery rhyme on the order of "Humpty Dumpty" and "Little Miss Muffet," recounting the tale of four little rats, three of whom die, one by one, after eating foods laced with poison. The fourth rat, desiring to join the other three in death, intentionally gorges himself; but he survives, merely growing plump in the process.

At another extreme, Pessoa created a Brazilian poet, Eduardo Lança, who is introduced in issue six of *O Palrador.* Lança's main contribution is a romantic poem entitled "Estátuas" [Statues], which retells the story of Lot's wife and draws a comparison between the tragic consequences of her glancing back at her homeland and the poet's looking back over his past. The poem bears the signature of Lança as well as the word "Terceira"—the name of the Azorean island where Pessoa briefly stayed. The same issue also contains a biographical sketch of Lança written by Luís António Congo, who is identified on the masthead as the assistant editor. This brief sketch is extremely significant in terms of Pessoa's mature work. In form and content, it is quite similar to the famous sketches he provided thirty years later in his letter on the major heteronyms. It gives us the date and place of Lança's birth (September 15, 1875, in Bahia, Brazil) and informs us that he came to Lisbon some years earlier to do business on behalf of a Brazilian firm. The note adds that Lança's first book, entitled *Impressões de Portugal* [Impressions of Portugal] and published in 1894, was written "num estilo belo e verdadeiramente português" [in a beautiful and truly Portuguese style]. It also remarks that Lança is the author of three other volumes of poetry, the most recent of which, *Os Meus Mitos* [My myths], published in 1900, is considered to be his best work.

The following issue of *O Palrador* contains a quatrain by Lança, entitled "Engima," as well as an announcement of his latest book of poems, entitled *Ao Luar* [By moonlight]. Like the sketch, this short announcement builds on the personality of Lança and attests to his authenticity by mixing fact with fiction: according to the note, Lança wrote sonnets in tribute to Tomás Ribeiro—an actual poet and statesman in Portugal, who had died the previous year. Although Lança's contributions to *O Palrador* are limited to two short poems, he stands out among all the other personae because of the world created for him through this note and the biographical sketch. In fact, he is probably the first instance of what Pessoa would ultimately call a heteronym, designed to create a "drama em gente" [drama in people] (3:1424).

The separate poets of the newspaper, much like the later heteronyms, have a tendency to merge or develop complex filiations with one another. For example, the most prolific poet and riddler in *O Palrador* is Dr. Pancrácio [Dr. Simpleton], whose special relationship to Pessoa "himself" is indicated on the masthead of the supplementary issue of *A Palavra*. Despite his name, Dr. Pancrácio is a clever punster, and, in the May 24 issue of *O Palrador,* he is put in charge of the section on charades. Here Dr. Pancrácio is also identified as the "antigo Pip" [former Pip]; and from this point on, he assumes an importance unique in comparison to Pessoa's other personalities. Not only is he the incarnation of Pip (a prominent poet and riddler in his own right, whose name subsequently disappears from the newspaper altogether) but, as of the July 5 issue of *O Palrador,* he is also acknowledged as the "literary director."

Among the many poems written by Dr. Pancrácio, the most significant is

"Quando Ela Passa" [When she passes], which is a longer version of one of the best-known works published in Fernando Pessoa's collected writings. Here is the short version of the poem, usually attributed to Pessoa "himself":

> Quando eu me sento à janela
> P'los vidros que a neve embaça
> Vejo a doce imagem dela
> Quando passa . . . passa . . . passa . . .
>
> Lançou-me a mágoa seu véu:—
> Menos um ser neste mundo
> E mais um anjo no céu.
>
> Quando eu me sento à janela
> P'los vidros que a neve embaça
> Julgo ver a imagem dela
> Que já não passa . . . não passa . . . (1:144)

> [When I sit at the window
> I see through the panes clouded by snow
> The sweet image of her
> When she passes . . . passes . . . passes . . .
>
> Grief casts its veil upon me:—
> One less being in this world
> And one more angel in heaven.
>
> When I sit at the window
> I think I see through the panes
> Clouded by snow her image
> That no longer passes . . . no longer passes . . .]

With the exception of a quatrain that he wrote as a young child, "Quando Ela Passa" was long regarded as Pessoa's first poem in Portuguese, and the considerable scholarly attention it has received is largely due to the fact that biographer João Gaspar Simões claimed that Pessoa was writing about his four-year-old stepsister, Madalena Henriqueta, who had died in South Africa in 1901. Because so few of Pessoa's poems reveal any personal information, this interpretation seems especially intriguing; it has been generally accepted and even appears in the introduction to his complete works (1:22). But Simões's hypothesis becomes questionable if one studies the longer version by Dr. Pancrácio in *O Palrador:*

Quando eu me sento à janela
P'los vidros qu'a neve embaça
Vejo a doce imagem d'ela
Quando passa . . . passa . . . passa . . .

N'esta escuridão tristonha
D'uma travessa sombria
Quando aparece risonha
Brilha mais qu'a luz do dia.

Quando está noite cerrada
E contemplo imagem sua
Que rompe a treva fechada
Como um reflexo da lua.

Penso ver o seu semblante
Com funda melancolia
Qu'o lábio embriagante
Não conheceu a alegria

E vejo curvado à dor
Todo o seu primeiro encanto
Comunica-mo o palor
As faces, aos olhos pranto.

Todos os dias passava
Por aquela estreita rua
E o palor que m'aterrava
Cada vez mais s'acentua

Um dia já não passou
O outro também já não
A sua ausência cavou
F'rida no meu coração

Na manhã do outro dia
Com o olhar amortecido
Fúnebre cortejo via
E o coração dolorido

Lançou-me em pesar profundo
Lançou-me a mágoa seu véu:—
Menos um ser n'este mundo
E mais um anjo no céu.

Depois o carro funéreo
Esse carro d'amargura
Entrou lá no cemetério
Eis ali a sepultura:

Epitáfio
Cristãos! Aqui jaz no pó da sepultura
Uma jovem filha da melancolia
O seu viver foi repleto d'amarguras
Seu rir foi pranto, dor sua alegria.

- - - . - - -

Quando eu me sento à janela
P'los vidros qu'a neve embaça
Julgo ver imagem d'ela
Que já não passa . . . não passa . . . [18]

[When I sit at the window
I see through the panes clouded by snow
Her sweet image
When she passes . . . passes . . . passes

In that sad darkness
Of a somber street
When she appears smiling
She shines more brightly than the light of day.

When it is nighttime
And I ponder her image
Which breaks through the solid darkness
Like the moon's recrudescence

I think I see her face
With its deep melancholy
And its intoxicating lips
That never knew happiness.

And I see all her youthful charm
Bent over in pain
Her cheeks imparting to me a pallor,
Her eyes bringing tears to mine.

Everyday she passed
Through that narrow street

And her terrifying pallor
Grew more intense each time.

One day she no longer passed by
Nor the next day
Her absence carved
A wound in my heart

On the morning of the following day
With a deadened look
I saw the funeral procession
And my heart ached

It caught and wounded me deeply
Grief cast its veil about me:—
One less being in this world
And one more angel in heaven.

Later the funeral carriage
That carriage of sorrow
Entered the cemetery beyond
Behold there her grave:

Epitaph
Christians! Here in the dust of the grave lies
A young daughter of melancholy
Whose life was replete with sorrow
Her laugh was tears, her happiness, grief.

- - - . - - -
When I sit at the window
I think I see through the panes clouded by snow
Her image that
No longer passes . . . no longer passes . . .]

The poem by Dr. Pancrácio was "published" ten days after the date attributed to the shorter, more elliptical version, and it gives us more information about the central figure. Obviously she is not a child, but a young woman, who walks by the poet's window every day and then ultimately passes in her funeral cortege. Far from being an actual person, she is a literary conceit, akin to the typically ethereal, melancholic, and virginal female found in much nineteenth-century romantic verse.

As is usually the case where Pessoa is concerned, "Quando Ela Passa" is best explained not in terms of the poet's autobiographical experience but in terms of his experience with other literature. He was surely aware of the popular Brazilian "ultraromantic" Álvares de Azevedo (also known as the "Brazilian Byron"), who composed numerous verses in which a woman's beauty and sensuality were directly related to her sleep or death. Azevedo's work harked back to the earliest forms of courtly love poetry, where the troubadour sings of his passion for a woman who is physically (i.e., socially) out of reach. But in Azevedo (as in Pessoa/Dr. Pancrácio), women were desirable only when kept at a distance and viewed from afar (or in a dream). This attraction to a woman's deathly pallor is also particularly evident in Edgar Allan Poe, whom Pessoa later translated into Portuguese.[19]

It seems likely that the composition of "Quando Ela Passa" was prompted by young Pessoa's interest in deliberately imitating or creating a pastiche of the ultraromantic tradition. That tradition was particularly strong in Portugal at the turn of the century, when romantic symbolists such as Augusto Gil were among the most widely read poets. Given the "mote e glosa" discussed earlier, we know that Pessoa was familiar with Gil's Versos, which contains a long poem entitled "Balada Outonal" [Autumn ballad] about a young, pale woman with grief-stricken eyes. The essential themes of "Quando Ela Passa" are all present in Gil's work, but there is an even closer connection with the slightly earlier Portuguese symbolist, António Nobre. In 1882, Nobre had published Só [Alone], the only book of his poetry to appear during his short lifetime. Só is filled with poems about death and disease—among them, "Pobre Tísica" [Poor consumptive], which appears in a section entitled "Elegias" [Elegies]. This poem begins "Quando ela passa à minha porta" [When she passes by my door], and it proceeds to describe the otherworldly attractiveness of a pale, sick young woman, whose "corpinho d'anjo, casto e inerme, / Vai ser amada pelo Verme, / Os bichos vão-na desfrutar" [small body of an angel, chaste and defenseless, / Is going to be made love to by the Worm, / The vermin are going to take pleasure in her].[20]

In an essay on Pessoa's poetry, the Portuguese scholar and poet Jorge de Sena has noted the similarity between the introductory line by Nobre and the title of Pessoa's poem, but he is basically concerned with proving that Nobre was the source of Pessoa's interest in octosyllabic verse.[21] The important point here is that Pessoa's poem is an overt *citation* of Nobre. Like the "mote e glosa" discussed previously, "Quando Ela Passa" begins with a "quotation" and then proceeds to "gloss" the image with lines that allude to still other sources. As a result of the elaboration or variation, we can perceive significant differences between Nobre and Pessoa: Nobre concentrates on the tragedy of consumptive illness, whereas Pessoa—like Poe,

Azevedo, and Gil—is voyeuristically caught up in the sensual effect of the woman's pallor.

Not content with these references to other poems, Pessoa went even further in creating variations for the newspaper version of "Quando Ela Passa." Prior to the appearance of either the short or long version of the poem, there appeared in the March 22 issue of *O Palrador* an "anecdote" written by Dr. Pancrácio entitled "Desapontamento" [Disappointment]. The piece begins as follows: "Era uma linda tarde de abril, domingo. Mas ainda mais linda era o pensamento que eu havia de ver a Rachel. Ela costumava passar por ali todos os dias, mas só aos domingos é que eu a podia ver, pois nos dias de semana estava àquela hora na repartição . . . Todo o homem que ama sabe que não há nada superior ao amor." [It was a lovely Sunday afternoon in April. But even more lovely was the thought that I was about to see Rachel. She was in the habit of passing by here every day, but it was only on Sundays that I saw her, for on weekdays at that hour, I was in the office . . . Every man who loves knows that there is nothing greater than love.] The narrator proceeds to describe how one day his beloved failed to appear and how very much he despaired. Upon hearing footsteps in the distance, he ran in their direction only to collide with a lottery ticket salesman, who was turning the corner where the woman normally appeared. Although disappointed, he purchased a ticket, and the following day he won the lottery. The story ends with the narrator proclaiming: "Enganei-me há pouco, meus amigos. Há uma coisa superior ao amor:—É a massa!!!" [I was wrong just a little while ago, my friends. There is something greater than love:—It's dough!!!][22]

"Desapontamento" and the two versions of "Quando Ela Passa" are interesting reworkings of a well-known literary motif: the woman seen from afar who becomes the object of the poet's desire. This motif was first posited in courtly love poetry and then repeated throughout literary history, especially in the necrophilic verse of the ultraromantics. Dr. Pancrácio's "Quando Ela Passa" imitates the tradition and at the same time works subtle variations on it; but the prose piece called "Desapontamento" has already placed the entire exercise in an ironic context, deflating it with a joke. Consequently, it is difficult to say whether Pessoa is emulating the verse of his predecessors, parodying it, or merely demonstrating that it represents a style that he can pick up "at will."

The most important and overlooked aspect of this poem and of the other examples I have mentioned is what it suggests about the act of writing for Pessoa. Quoting Kristeva, we might say that all his work was "a [conscious] reading of the anterior literary corpus," and his various compositions represent "an absorption of and a reply to" not just one but several other texts.[23] As a consequence of his love of parody, pastiche, and imitation, he created the later heteronyms, who provide him with a complete imaginary world and who function as a kind of tradition—a series of texts that play off against one another and against literary history in general. The heteronymous poems are, of course, more ambitious and more complex achievements than the verses described in this chapter; even so, they derive from many of the same procedures, elaborated into a universe of styles. It seems clear that, like many other figures of the high-modernist generation, Pessoa was preserving or constructing an elite literary heritage through a process of imitation and quotation. In formal and philosophical terms, however, he was also a deconstructionist, somewhat along the lines of Joyce or Borges. Throughout his later work, he dissolved the poetic self into myriad voices, confounding the philosophically untenable distinction between imitation and originality. By creating what he called "a fusion of past elements," he paradoxically generated a kind of metapoetry that was both versatile and distinctly his own.

2

Nationalism, Modernism, and the Formation of Pessoa's Aesthetic

In August 1905, at the age of seventeen, Pessoa moved away from his family home in Durban and departed for Lisbon. There he lived for a while with two aunts on the Rua da Bela Vista (the same address that appears on Alexander Search's calling card), and he never left Portugal again. He enrolled in the University of Lisbon, first in philosophy, then in literature,[1] but he abandoned his studies following a student strike in 1907 against the unpopular royalist prime minister, João Franco. In August that same year, Pessoa's paternal grandmother died, leaving him a small bequest. He invested the money in a printing press which he bought in the town of Portalegre in the Alentejo, a sparsely populated region of vast plains in the interior of Portugal. In the fall of 1907, he opened a print shop in the center of Lisbon under the name "Empresa Ibis" [Ibis Enterprise],[2] but the venture never got off the ground. Following this failed attempt as an entrepreneur, he made use of his knowledge of English, French, and Portuguese, as well as the technical training he had acquired in South Africa, and hired himself out as a commercial translator—a humble profession which he practiced for the rest of his life. Although he earned very little, the job's flexible work hours provided him with the time he needed to write,[3] and within five years he became an influential figure in the world of Portuguese literary periodicals.

Between 1910 and his death in 1935, Pessoa also witnessed a series of important events in Portuguese social and political history: the demise of the monarchy, the establishment of the Republic, the rise and fall of Sidónio Pais, and the ultimate creation of the Estado Novo [New State]. His writing in the beginning of the period was strongly affected by a wave of revolutionary nationalism that swept across the country; at the same time, however, he was an artistic internationalist and a key figure in the development of Portuguese literary modernism. The twin influences of nationalism and modernism—one looking back to "native" sources, the other looking forward to a cosmopolitan sensibility—helped to shape not only his aesthetic theories but also his attitudes toward history. Similar to William Butler Yeats in Ireland but with significant local differences, his work manifests contradictory impulses that are held in a productive tension. On one hand, he attempted to define an "authentic" national tradition, expressing nostalgia for the epic glories of a Lusitanian empire; on the other hand, he was keenly aware of vanguard poetic movements, and he participated in the worldwide drive to "make it new." The Janus-faced quality of his thinking probably contributed to the development of the heteronyms and at the same time enabled him to manipulate different stylistic tendencies within single poems, where he was able to reconcile powerful oppositions.

Saudosismo and the Literary Avant-Garde

Critic Marjorie Perloff has remarked that the internationalist spirit of the European avant-garde in the years prior to World War I was short-lived and that the "poignancy" of the era derives from a "tension between cosmopolitanism and a stubborn nationalism."[4] In the case of Portugal, such tensions lasted far beyond the brief moment of the *avant guerre,* although they were especially evident during Pessoa's formative period as a writer. When he left the country as child in 1896, the monarchy was in financial and moral crisis.[5] The government's attempt to occupy new territories in Africa, blocked by the British "ultimatum" in 1890, was an embarrassing blow for a once-powerful country that prided itself on its long-standing alliance with England. Opposition to the monarchy, in the form of republicanism or bourgeois revolution, steadily increased. In 1891, republicans attempted a rebellion from a military garrison in Oporto; although the revolt was quickly put down, the action impacted on the country's already unstable political life, and dissension and parliamentary gridlock soon became the norm.[6] A large foreign debt forced Portugal to declare bankruptcy in 1892 and again in 1902. In 1907, King Carlos closed Parliament and gave his new premier, João Franco, dictatorial powers. On January 28 of the following year, Franco deported republican leaders as well as some monarchists who were charged with plotting a revolt. On February 1, the king and his eldest son were assassinated by republican sympathizers. According to historian Tom Gallagher, "200,000 people turned out for the funeral of the assassins, while the king's burial was a much quieter affair."[7] After Franco's resignation, the young and inexperienced new king, Dom Manuel II, who had a much larger military, was unable to stop a republican takeover. Conceding defeat, he boarded a ship and sailed to England; and on October 5, 1910, after more than seven centuries of monarchical rule, the First Portuguese Republic was proclaimed.

For the majority of middle- and working-class Portuguese, including the twenty-two-year-old Pessoa, the republic promised a better economic future. As historian Alves da Veiga wrote glowingly at the time, "The Portuguese Republic has before it a great mission to carry out—to create a new Fatherland, to build a modern people."[8] The republic was also linked with the myth of *sebastianismo*—a popular belief that Portugal would be saved and its greatness restored by the "return" or historical repetition of values represented by its lost king, Sebastião.[9] According to historian Douglas Wheeler, "[L]ong after persons claiming to be Sebastian had ceased to appear . . . [there] was a hope for national revival founded on the belief that a person, a personal hero, a great man would make all the difference."[10] For a unique moment, the republic seemed to stand in place of "the great man," representing the strength of the Portuguese bourgeoisie and offering something like a messianic appeal.

Despite his many years away from Portugal, Pessoa was caught up in the spirit of patriotism and Sebastianism that fueled the republican cause.[11] He was also attracted to the idea of revolution because it had sources in an anti-Catholic movement. Many republicans were opposed to the rule of the church, and some came from the ranks of Protestant or Masonic organizations. For his part, Pessoa had been raised in a Catholic family, but his upbringing had not been especially devout; indeed, during the formative years of his literary career, he adopted a kind of symbolist mysticism as a substitute for organized religion.

Even after the revolution, Pessoa continued to be influenced by the nationalism and vague spirituality of "republican Sebastianism," and his work was increasingly affected by a new movement called *saudosismo*, which sought to effect a cultural revival on the order of the Renaissance. Headed by the poet Teixeira de Pascoaes, the movement took its name from the Portuguese word *saudade,* an untranslatable term whose closest English equivalents are "longing" or "nostalgia."[12]

The idea of *saudade* is pervasive in Portuguese culture and, like Sebastianism, has become an aspect of the national sensibility, manifesting itself in various historical periods and contexts. A paradoxically revolutionary yet reactionary tendency, it became fundamental in the literature and philosophy of the *saudosistas,* or literary Sebastianists, who looked to Portugal's past as a source of pride and hope for the country's rebirth.[13] Because *saudade* was considered an exclusively Portuguese trait, it served as an emblem or symbol for the country's *ressurgimento* [resurgence]—a term that came to connote the greatness ascribed to Portugal's "Golden Age." In the words of Teixeira de Pascoaes: "a alma portuguesa gerou nas suas entranhas penetradas por uma luz celeste, a *Saudade,* a nebulosa do futuro Canto imortal, o Verbo do novo mundo português . . . É na Saudade *revelada* que existe a razão da nossa Renascença; nela ressurgiremos, porque ela é a própria Renascença original e criadora" [the Portuguese soul engendered in its inner being penetrated by a celestial light, *Saudade,* the nebulous spirit of the future immortal Song, the Word of the new Portuguese world . . . It is in the Saudade *revealed* that the reason for our Renaissance exists; in it we will resurge, because it is the original and creative Renaissance itself].[14]

Saudosismo's invocation of a Renaissance, or, in Pascoaes' words, "tirar das fontes originárias da vida uma nova vida" [to pull from the originating sources of life a new life], strongly appealed to Pessoa, who had a sense of national pride as well as Sebastianist inclinations.[15] In 1912, he published the first of several essays in which he praised the originality and patriotism of the new generation's writings—in particular the poetry of Pascoaes, whom he portrayed as a kind of prophet. Entitled "A Nova Poesia Portuguesa Sociologicamente Considerada" [The new Portuguese poetry considered sociologically], the article appeared in *A Águia* [The eagle], the official review of the Oporto-based *saudosistas,* and it provoked a mild literary furor because of Pessoa's reference to a "Supra-Camões," an epic poet who would usher into Portugal a period of national and literary greatness or "ressurgimento assombroso" [astounding resurgence] (2:1153). In effect, Pessoa was extending the "great man" idea of social or political Sebastianism into the literary sphere and perhaps announcing his own desire to become a savior.

Even at this stage, however, Pessoa's aesthetics were contradictory. There is no such thing as an essential or natural Portuguese identity, and despite Pessoa's many claims to the contrary, the *saudosistas* were as much indebted to recent trends in continental literature as to the national past. Thus, in a later essay, "A Nova Poesia Portuguesa no seu Aspecto Psicológico" [The new Portuguese poetry in its psychological aspect], which also appeared in *A Águia* in 1912, Pessoa described the artistic program of the *saudosistas* in terms of three highly abstract principles: vagueness, subtlety, and complexity—ideas that were also central to French symbolism (2:1174). Here he singled out verses by Pascoaes as well as two other *saudosistas,* Mário Beirão and Jaime Cortesão, offering them as examples of the best of the *saudosista* aesthetic. Pessoa described this aesthetic in ro-

A cover for *A Águia*, the journal of the Portuguese *saudosista* movement (1912).

mantically philosophical terms as "transcendentalismo panteísta" [pantheistic transcendentalism], a system involving the fusion of totally opposite elements, the result of which he associated with the formation of a new Lusitanian soul (2:1189, 1194).

As the Portuguese critic Jacinto do Prado Coelho has observed, Pessoa's tendency to announce new schools or poetic ideologies seems to prefigure the arrival of the vanguard journal *Orpheu*, an important publication inaugurated in 1915 by a younger generation of artists and poets, including Pessoa, Mário de Sá-Carneiro, Almada Negreiros, Luís de Montalvor, and the Brazilian Ronald de Carvalho, which is usually regarded as the official beginning of Portuguese modernism. To paraphrase the argument of the German scholar Georg Rudolf Lind, we might say that Pessoa was both encouraging nationalistic *saudosismo* and opening developments in twentieth-century art.[16]

It soon became apparent that Pessoa was moving along a different path from his *saudosista* compatriots, who were somewhat suspicious of literary and artistic developments outside Portugal. That group was often xenophobic, as we can see in a seminal article published in *A Águia* in 1912 by Teixeira de Pascoaes: "Sim: a alma portuguesa existe, e o seu perfil é eterno e original. Revelemo-la agora a todos os portugueses, na sua maior parte afastados dela, pelas más influências literárias, políticas e religiosas vindas do estrangeiro" [Yes: the Portuguese soul exists, and its profile is eternal and original. Let us now reveal it to all the Portuguese, for the most part removed from it by the bad literary, political and religious influences from abroad]. This traditionalist attitude was also espoused by António Sardinha, the leader of the fascist organization Integralismo Lusitano (1914–1926), who contended that foreign influences were responsible for Portugal's decline.[17] By contrast, Pessoa was intellectually cosmopolitan; he kept abreast of the most recent literary movements in Europe through newspapers like *O Diário dos Açores,* which published Marinetti's *Futurist Manifesto* in 1909; *O Rebate* [The rebuttal], which reviewed the most recent theatrical events in Berlin, Paris, and Rome; and the magazine *Ilustração Portuguesa,* which reproduced cubist and futurist paintings.[18] Meanwhile, his friend Mário de Sá-Carneiro wrote to him regularly from Paris, and his artist-friend Santa Rita Pintor returned to Lisbon from France with the ideas for translating Marinetti into Portuguese and launching a futurist literary review.

Pessoa was attracted to these avant-garde developments, but in many respects he remained faithful to what he called a "Lusitanian or *saudosista*" creed. He continued writing nationalistic lyrics, associated with traditional "Portuguese" themes, all the while finding ways to integrate them within a modernist aesthetic. One of his poems from 1913, "Impressões do Crepúsculo" [Impressions of twilight], which was published a year later in the literary review *A Renascença* [The Renaissance], helps to demonstrate how he combined *fin-de-siècle* nationalism with the emerging international modernism. This poem was Pessoa's first verse to appear in print since his 1902 "mote e glosa," and, like the earlier publication, it consists of a two-part variation on a familiar theme. The first part is a rhymed ballad, executed in a late romantic style; and the second is a free-verse experiment in poetic inner monologue, resembling the impressionism of Mallarmé or Valéry. The juxtaposition of two such distinctive styles has the effect of a deliberate clash or conflict:

I
Ó sino da minha aldeia,
Dolente na tarde calma,
Cada tua badalada
Soa dentro da minh'alma.

E é tão lento o teu soar,
Tão como triste da vida,
Que já a primeira pancada
Tem um som de repetida.

Por mais que me tanjas perto
Quando passo triste e errante,
És para mim como um sonho—
Soas me sempre distante . . .

A cada pancada tua,
Vibrante no céu aberto,
Sinto mais longe o passado,
Sinto a saudade mais perto.

II
Pauis de roçarem ânsias pela minh'alma em ouro . . .
Dobre longínquo de Outros Sinos . . . Empalidece o louro
Trigo na cinza do poente . . . Corre um fio carnal por minh'alma . . .
Tão sempre a mesma, a Hora! . . . Balouçar de cimos de palma . . .
Silêncio que as folhas fitam em nós . . . Outono delgado
Dum canto de vaga ave . . . Azul esquecido em estagnado . . .
Oh que mudo grito de ânsia põe garras na Hora!
Que pasmo de mim anseia por outra coisa que o que chora!
Estendo as mãos para além, mas ao estendê-las já vejo
Que não é aquilo que quero aquilo que desejo . . .
Címbalos de Imperfeição . . . Ó tão antiguidade
A Hora expulsa de si-Tempo! . . . Onda de recuo que invade
O meu abandonar-me a mim-próprio até desfalecer,
E recordar tanto o Eu presente que me sinto esquecer! . . .
Fluído de auréola, transparente de Foi, oco de ter-se . . .
O Mistério sabe-me a eu ser outro . . . Luar sobre o não conter-se . . .

A sentinela é hirta—a lança que finca no chão
É mais alta do que ela . . . Pra que é tudo isto? . . . Dia chão . . .
Trepadeiras de despropósito lambendo de Hora os Aléns . . .
Horizontes fechando os olhos ao espaço em que são elos de erro . . .
Fanfarras de ópios de silêncios futuros . . . Longes trens . . .
Portões vistos longe . . . através das árvores . . . tão de ferro! . . .[19]

I
[Oh bell of my village,
Dolorous in the calm afternoon,
Each one of your peals,
Rings deep within my soul.

And so slow is your ringing,
As if so sad of life,
That the first stroke already
Sounds like a repetition.

For as much as you toll near me
When errant and sad I pass,
To me you are like a dream—
Always sounding distant.

For every one of your rings
Vibrating in the open sky,
I feel the past farther away,
I feel a longing closer by.

II
Quagmires grazing qualms of anguish through my soul in gold . . .
Distant tolling of Other Bells . . . The gold wheat
Pales in the cinders of sunset . . . A carnal thread runs through my
    soul . . .
So always the same, the Hour! . . . Swaying tops of palms . . .
Silence that leaves stare into us . . . Slim autumn
Of a vague bird's song . . . Forgotten blue, stagnant . . .
Oh what mute cry of agony claws at the Hour!
What wonder in me yearns for something else than that which
    cries!
I extend my hands to the beyond, but on extending them I now see
That what I want is not what I desire . . .

Cymbals of Imperfection . . . Oh so much antiquity
Expels the Hour from itself-Time! . . . Receding wave that invades
My self abandoned by me until I faint,
And the present I remember so much that I feel myself forgetting! . . .
Fluid of aureole, transparent of Was, hollow from having itself . . .
The Mystery knows me to be another . . . Moonlight over the
    uncontainable . . .
The sentinel is rigid—the lance driven into the ground
Is taller than he . . . What is this all for? . . . Day ground . . .
Climbing vines of irrelevance licking every Hour the Beyonds . . .
Horizons closing eyes to the space in which errors are linked
    together . . .
Opium fanfares of future silences . . . Long trains . . .
Large gates seen afar . . . through the trees . . . so very iron! . . .]

The first poem in the two-part sequence, which I shall refer to as "Ó
Sino," is composed of a series of rhymed quatrains in the form of a *redondilha*. Like so many of the poems Pessoa would subsequently write
under his own name, it is strongly reminiscent of the celebrated romantic,
Almeida Garrett, whose volume *Folhas Caídas* [Fallen leaves] (1853)
Pessoa greatly admired. A liberal and political exile during the 1830s' civil
war in Portugal, Garrett was especially popular among the *saudosistas*,
chiefly because of his desire to create a national literature. Garrett was also
a skillful manipulator of internal rhyme and various musical effects, including alliteration and onomatopoeia. In "Ó Sino," Pessoa is clearly imitating
this style: consider the phrases "cada tua badalada" and "A cada pancada
tua," which resemble Garrett's most musical poem, "Pescador da Barca
Bela" [Fisherman of the beautiful boat]. At the same time, Pessoa's central
image of the village bell brings to mind António Nobre's melancholic "Os
Sinos" [The bells] (1892); and his title "Impressões do Crepúsculo" points
toward Pascoaes, who often used the word *crepúsculo* (as well as a host
of synonymous terms such as *nevoeiro* [mist], *sonho* [dream], and *ermo*
[desert]) to convey the dreamy mood characteristic of much *saudosista*
verse.[20]
    The second part of the poem, which I shall refer to as "Pauis," echoes the
first in certain ways but is a more vanguard attempt to achieve the "vagueness, subtlety and complexity" that Pessoa admired in Pascoaes. This section is hallucinatory and synaesthetic, employing such disparate images as
"quagmires" and "the distant tolling of Other Bells" to suggest the poet's
agonized, swooning desire for an indefinable other. In common with much

French symbolist verse, it resembles a drug-induced dream in which cryptic and apparently incomparable elements mingle together. Idealized or personified terms such as Time, Hour, Mystery, and Beyond are coupled with phrases that connote fluidity and transparency ("onda de recuo," "fluído de auréola," "transparente de Foi"), as if the poem were trying to blend mutability with transcendence and sensuality with Platonic essences.

For Pessoa's biographer João Gaspar Simões, the style of "Pauis" represented an attempt at an "intellectualization of *saudosismo*," while for the critic Nuno Júdice it signaled the beginnings of Portuguese modernism.[21] In fact, "Pauis" became the model and inspiration for *paúlismo*—a short-lived avant-garde movement led by Pessoa and taken up by Sá-Carneiro and others. Shortly after receiving a copy of "Pauis," Sá-Carneiro wrote to Pessoa from Paris in the breathless tones of an enraptured aesthete who has recognized a kindred spirit: "Quanto aos PAUIS . . . Eu sinto-os, eu *compreendo-os,* e acho-os simplesmente uma coisa maravilhosa . . . É álcool doirado, é chama louca, perfume de ilhas misteriosas o que você pôs nesse excerto admirável, onde abundam as garras." [As for QUAGMIRES . . . I feel them, I *understand them,* and I find them simply marvelous . . . What you put in this admirable excerpt, where claws abound, is golden alcohol, a mad flame, perfume from mysterious isles].[22]

Curiously, however, despite the obvious historical importance of "Pauis" and the considerable critical and scholarly attention that the separate parts of the poem have received, no one has ever commented on Pessoa's decision to link the two different styles under a single title. Critical neglect of this issue is probably due to the simple fact that, after Pessoa's death, the organizers of his papers treated "Ó Sino" and "Pauis" as two unrelated texts, placing them apart from each other in the collected works and attributing the title "Impressões do Crepúsculo" to "Pauis" alone.

When the two parts are grouped together in their original form, they demonstrate that Pessoa was equally drawn to Portuguese nationalism and to a new continental literature. Indeed, the two distinct styles seem to foreshadow the technique of multiple voices or heteronyms in his subsequent work. "Ó Sino" is typical of a great many verses written by Pessoa "himself," whereas "Pauis" seems to belong with two other uncharacteristically long poems that he composed at about the same time: "Hora Absurda" [Absurd hour] and "Chuva Oblíqua" [Oblique rain], the latter of which anticipates the self-reflexive and often anguished poetry of his modernist heteronym, Álvaro de Campos.[23] Significantly, the two sections of "Impressões do Crepúsculo" appeared virtually on the eve of Pessoa's decision to write in the form of heteronyms.

These implications aside, how shall we describe the purely *formal* or structural relation between the two parts of "Impressões do Crepúsculo"? There would seem to be at least three possible ways of answering the question. The first is to regard "Ó Sino" and "Pauis" as representing completely different tendencies of Pessoa's work, separating them from each other and discussing them as more or less distinct poems. This is the strategy adopted by Pessoa's editors, but it disregards the fact that the verses were initially published together and were intended as a single work. A second possibility is to regard the two parts of the poem as a sign that Pessoa was moving away from a traditional Portuguese romanticism, declaring his sympathy with the symbolist or protomodernist aesthetic; in other words, we can read the second half of the poem as a kind of cancellation of the first, or as a stage in Pessoa's "progress" toward a new style. This strategy seems equally problematic, because it treats the two parts of the poem hierarchically. In point of fact, Pessoa never rejected the techniques represented by "Ó Sino," and he continued to write similar verse throughout his life.

The third way of understanding the poem, and the one more in keeping with the development of the heteronyms, is to emphasize the dialectical relation between the two parts. Like the "mote e glosa," "Impressões do Crepúsculo" gives us a theme and variation, meanwhile representing two phases in the history of literary fashion; but it also has the feeling of a montage, setting its parts in conflict with each other and allowing them a certain autonomy. As in Hegelian dialectics, the total poem is more than the sum of its two parts, and the synthesis of the whole does not negate or cancel either half. Instead, the poem preserves its different voices, carrying the first one forward into a new relation through a process of sublation or *Aufhebung*.[24]

Pessoa briefly mentioned a similar artistic process in his very first essay in *A Águia,* attributing its fundamental principles to Hegel (2:1189).[25] As we have seen in the previous chapter, he later employed the word "constructiveness" to signify a "fusion of past elements" out of which a new Portuguese literature or "alma nova Lusitana" would emerge. In both the early essay in *A Águia* and in the argument about "constructiveness," Pessoa was attempting to describe a relation between past and present that would overcome contradiction by means of a dialectical and nonlinear form. This strategy enabled him to take an artistic (and implicitly political) position that was neither reactionary nor completely in sympathy with the utopian wing of the European avant-garde. It also provided him with an opportunity to imitate different voices, setting them in contrast with one another without committing himself to a single style or a master rhetoric.

"I Am Merely I": Futurism and Traditionalism in *Orpheu*

Pessoa's particular styles of multivocality can be heard in his various contributions (written under different names) to *Orpheu* and *Portugal Futurista*. The former review is generally regarded as Portugal's earliest attempt to create an avant-garde publication, although the furor surrounding the appearance of its first issue in March 1915 made it seem more radical than it actually was.[26] Like many publications in England and America during this same period, *Orpheu* showed a certain awareness of movements like futurism and cubism, combined with traditionalist or antidemocratic political inclinations; indeed, republican officials were convinced that it was an instrument of protest connected with the right-wing monarchist party.[27] The very title of the review suggested its grounding in classical literature and one of its "scandalous" offerings—Sá-Carneiro's "16"—was actually a symbolist poem, filled with dreamy imagery and romantic references to the "Ânsia" [Anguish] of the poet's "Alma" [Soul]. Notwithstanding its overriding debt to the *fin de siècle*, however, *Orpheu* was also a younger generation's attempt to define itself, giving expression to a wide range of emerging literary sensibilities. In a letter to the Portuguese philosopher Sampaio Bruno in March 1915, Pessoa explained that *Orpheu* was a synthesis of different personalities and styles, a "corrente original . . . que transcende essas, citadas, correntes anteriores" [original current . . . that transcends those other, cited, previous currents] (2:195).

As a member of the *Orpheu* collective and coeditor of the journal's second issue, Pessoa actively solicited materials from literary friends to insure a feeling of eclecticism, and his own writing reflected a willingness to experiment with a variety of styles. In the first issue he published his symbolist-inspired "static drama," *O Marinheiro* [The sailor]. By contrast, his other contribution to the same issue, "Ode Triunfal," signed by "Álvaro de Campos," written in "London, 1914," and "published by Fernando Pessoa," is an irreverent and ostentatiously avant-garde composition in which the eroticization of the relationship between man and machine seems to parody both Whitman and Marinetti:

Ó fábricas, ó laboratórios, ó *music-halls*, ó Luna-Parks.
Ó couraçados, ó pontes, ó docas flutuantes—
Na minha mente turbulenta e incandescida
Possuo-vos como a uma mulher bela,
Completamente vos possuo como a uma mulher bela que não se
   ama,
Que se encontra casualmente e se acha interessantíssima.

. . .

Eu podia morrer triturado por um motor
Com o sentimento de deliciosa entrega duma mulher possuída.
Atirem-me para dentro das fornalhas!
Metam-me debaixo dos comboios!
Espanquem-me a bordo de navios!
Masoquismo através de maquinismos!
Sadismo de não sei quê moderno e eu e barulho! (1:881–82)

[Oh factories, oh laboratories, oh music-halls, oh Luna-Parks,
Oh battleships, oh bridges, oh floating docks—
In my turbulent and incandescent mind
I possess you as if you were a beautiful woman,
I possess you completely as if you were a beautiful woman whom
    one doesn't love,
Whom one casually encounters and finds extremely interesting.

. . .

I could die triturated by a motor
With the feeling of delicious surrender of a woman possessed.
Throw me into the furnaces!
Place me beneath the trains!
Spank me on board ships!
Masochism through mechanisms!
Sadism of I know not what modern and I and noise!]

Looked at together, O Marinheiro and "Ode Triunfal" form an interesting split between Pessoa's "own" fin-de-siècle persona and that of Álvaro de Campos, whose identity is linked with modern times. Both tendencies were in play throughout Portuguese literary culture in the period, although the modernist style dominates the second issue of Orpheu. Pessoa's contribution to the issue, a six-part "intersectionist" poem entitled "Chuva Oblíqua" [Oblique rain], borrows some of its motifs from symbolism but has a distinctly unorthodox feel.[28] Meanwhile, the thirty-eight-page-long ode by Pessoa's heteronym the "engineer" Álvaro de Campos, "Ode Marítima" [Maritime ode], is, like his "Ode Triunfal," filled with onomatopoeic effects that verge on Marinetti's "words at liberty."

Notice, however, that even within an ostensibly modern work like "Ode Marítima," we can find powerful oppositions between old and new. Standing on a Lisbon dock and looking out to the sea, Campos thinks of the place as a "saudade de pedra" [longing of stone], a "Grande Cais donde partimos em Navios-Nações" [Great Dock from which we part in Nation-Ships] (1:892). He begins to fantasize about the past and longs to "despir de mim" [divest myself] (1:901). Casting off his "traje de civilizado" [civilized suit] and "brandura de acções" [gentleness of action] (1:901), he imaginatively joins the slave traders and sailors of the days of the empire. In its oneiric passages, "Ode Marítima" evokes the boisterous, violent, seafaring adventures of pirates and is replete with the sounds of sinister laughter ("EH-EH-EH-EH-EH-EH-EH-EH-EH-EH"), drunken song ("FIFTEEN MEN ON THE DEAD MAN'S CHEST / YO-HO-HO AND A BOTTLE OF RUM!"), and battle ("ahó-ó-ó-ó-ó-ó-ó-ó-ó-ó——yyyy . . . / Schooner ahó-ó-ó-ó-ó-ó-ó-ó-ó-ó-ó——yyy . . .") (see 1:891–947). Designed to imitate the ocean during a storm, it contains a chaotic vision in which the poet declares that he is "o pirata-resumo de toda a pirataria no seu auge, / E a vítima-síntese, mas de carne e osso, de todos os piratas do mundo!" [the pirate-summary of all the piracy at its peak, / And the victim-synthesis, but of flesh and bone, of all the pirates in the world!] (1:905). Like the calm after the storm, the poem concludes on a restrained, introspective note, with the description of a steamer slowly sailing out of sight, and the poet's "awakening" to find himself alone on a dock, surrounded by modern hoists and cranes.

Somewhat like "Ó Sino" and "Pauis," which I have described earlier, the "Ode Marítima" alternates between Apollonian and Dionysian states of consciousness; and in its most delirious and technically vanguard moments, it reveals Pessoa's ambivalence toward futurist experimentation. The rational and practical Campos is preoccupied with machines and steamships only during the quotidian moments of his life. In his daydreams or fantasies, which have been compared to those of the American poet Hart Crane, he regresses historically to an antiquarian world of schooners and pirates. The poem becomes "primal" in various senses: in its use of a frankly masochistic and homoerotic imagery; in its break with rational syntax; and most of all in its maritime visions, which can be associated with Portugal's heroic past. Campos therefore seems a paradox: a daringly new kind of poet, he is also intensely nostalgic for a preindustrial age.

Pessoa and the other writers associated with *Orpheu* were frequently characterized as futurists, but they were never truly in the futurist camp. Pessoa tried to make this clear in June 1915, when he composed a letter to the *Diário de Notícias* under the name of Campos:

> Falar em futurism, quer a propósito do 1.º n.º "*Orpheu,*" quer a propósito do livro do Sr. Sá-Carneiro, é a coisa mais disparatada que se pode imaginar. Nenhum futurista tragaria o "*Orpheu.*" O "*Or-*

pheu" seria, para um futurista, uma lamentável demonstração de espírito obscurantista e reaccionário . . .

. . . Englobar os colaboradores do "*Orpheu*" no futurismo é nem
sequer saber dizer disparates, o que é lamentabilíssimo. (2:1099–
1100)

[To speak of futurism, whether in relation to the 1st no. of *Orpheu,*
or in relation to the book by Mr. Sá-Carneiro, is the most preposter-
ous thing one can imagine. No futurist would swallow *Orpheu.* For a
futurist, *Orpheu* would be a lamentable demonstration of an obscu-
rant and reactionary spirit . . .

. . . To place the contributors of *Orpheu* together within futurism
is not even to know how ludicrous it sounds, which is in itself highly
lamentable.]

Campos then proceeded to elaborate on the distinctive qualities of his own
work:

A minha *Ode Triunfal,* no 1.º número do "*Orpheu,*" é a única
coisa que se aproxima do futurismo. Mas aproxima-se pelo assunto
que me inspirou, não pela realização—e em arte a forma de realizar é
que caracteriza e distingue as correntes e as escolas.

Eu, de resto, nem sou interseccionista (ou paúlico) nem futurista.
Sou eu, apenas eu, preocupado apenas comigo e com as minhas sensações. (2:1100)

[My "Ode Triunfal," in the 1st number of *Orpheu,* is the only
thing that approaches futurism. But it approaches futurism through
the subject matter that inspired me, not by the form—and in art the
form of realizing is what characterizes and distinguishes currents and
schools.

I'm neither intersectionist (or paulic) nor futurist. I am, merely I,
concerned simply with myself and with my sensations.]

At first glance, Campos's remarks seem to be an accurate description of
Orpheu as a whole. It is certainly true that the Portuguese movement was
philosophically idealist and never "anti-art" in the fashion of radical futurism. It is also true that Pessoa was interested in what his heteronym Campos describes as "excessive subjectivity." Despite the fact that Pessoa was

intrigued by the avant-garde, all of his writings from the period suggest that he remained committed to romantic individualism and an aesthetic of private sensation. The problem here is that the romantic ideology has been thrown into crisis by the invention of a nonexistent poet called "Álvaro de Campos." How can we possibly take at face value the statement: "I am, merely I," after we have discovered that Pessoa is playing tricks with identity?

Clearly, the heteronyms foreshadow our own, postmodern interest in "the death of the subject," and in that respect they seem "advanced," closer to the late twentieth century than anything produced by the historical avant-garde. But it is important to emphasize that Pessoa was not attempting to break completely with the past. In several of his other guises, he tried to make distinctions between *Orpheu* and futurism—as we can see from another document that he wrote at about the same time, signed with the name of the philosopher-heteronym, "António Mora": "Devo a minha compreensão dos literatos de "*Orpheu*" a uma leitura aturada sobretudo dos gregos, que habilitam quem os saiba ler a não ter pasmo de coisa nenhuma. Da Grécia Antiga vê-se o mundo inteiro, o passado como o futuro, a tal altura emerge, dos menores cumes das outras civilizações, o seu alto píncaro de glória criadora" [I owe my comprehension of the literati of *Orpheu* to a persistent reading especially of the Greeks, who teach those who know how to read not to be astounded by anything. One sees the whole world from Ancient Greece, the past as well as the future, at such height emerges, from the smallest peaks of other civilizations, its pinnacle of creative glory] (2:1320). In this case Pessoa seems to be speaking as a classicist rather than as a romantic. Even so, his separate personae remain consistent in their uneasy or negative attitude toward futurism.[29] Ultimately, the different voices help to confirm Pessoa's belief that *Orpheu* represented a *multiplicity* of styles which together formed a synthesis.

Perhaps Pessoa's greatest quarrel with futurism lay in the fact it wanted to declare that the past was dead and that art had died along with it.[30] For Pessoa, the past (meaning, in this case, traditional art and hierarchical Portuguese nationalism) was vital to the process out of which a new literary movement would emerge. By 1916, Pessoa had dropped the name *interseccionismo* for this movement, and was calling it *sensacionismo* [sensationism]. In a long letter written in English for a British publisher, he mapped out the fundamentals of the movement, which he classified as "a new species of Weltanschauung": The sensationists, he explained, "descend from three older movements—French 'symbolism', Portuguese transcendentalist pantheism, and the jumble of senseless and contradictory things of which futurism, cubism and the like are occasional expressions, though, to be exact, we descend more from the spirit than from the letter of these" (3:192). Once again, Pessoa acknowledges a variety of sources, some "native" and others continental, meanwhile trying to disassociate himself from too close an affiliation with the avant-garde. Later in the same document, he returns to futurism and cubism and further minimizes their influence:

As to our influences from the modern movement which embraces cubism and futurism, it is rather owing to the suggestions we received from them, than to the substance of their works properly speaking.

We have intellectualized their processes. The decomposition of the model they realise (because we have been influenced, not by their literature, if they have anything resembling literature, but by their pictures), we have carried into what we believe to be the proper sphere of that decomposition—*not things, but our sensations of things.* (3:193)

This quest for a sort of literary impressionism based on a doctrine of "sensations" was relatively short-lived. In 1917, two years after *Orpheu*'s second and final issue was published,[31] many of the same individuals who had formed that journal participated in *Portugal Futurista,* a review that bears a strong resemblance to Wyndham Lewis and Ezra Pound's *Blast.* Like *Orpheu,* however, *Portugal Futurista* was an eclectic, cosmopolitan publication. It contains a good many avant-garde works, including translations from Marinetti, Umberto Boccioni, and Carlo Carrá; reproductions of futurist paintings by Santa Rita Pintor and Amadeu de Souza Cardoso; manifestos by Almada Negreiros and Álvaro de Campos; and poetry by Apollinaire and Blaise Cendrars. Nevertheless, Pessoa's "own" poems for the journal—"A Múmia" [The mummy] and "Ficções do Interlúdio" [Fictions of the interlude]—are fairly traditional compositions, especially when compared to the bombastic "Ultimatum" by his heteronym Campos, which begins: "Mandado de despejo aos mandarins da Europa! Fora" [Eviction notice to the mandarins of Europe! Get out] followed by the proclamation "Vou indicar o caminho!" [I'll show you the way!].[32]

In Pessoa's decision to write under different names for vanguard journals and in the internal tensions of all his later work, we can perceive an ambivalence toward modernity and a dissatisfaction with any idea of linear progress or simple rupture with the past. His solution to the contradiction was to make "lost history" reemerge in a new form. By this means, he could

The cover of *Portugal Futurista* (1917).

retain a sense of Portuguese identity and at the same time create a fundamentally modernist aesthetic, characterized by the simultaneous presence of different styles. As we shall see in subsequent chapters, the mingling of tradition and experimentation in Pessoa's mature work resembles nearly all the major writers of the high-modernist generation (especially authors such as Eliot and Yeats), who tried to maintain a link with classical or national tradition while instigating a literary revolution.

The Politics of Contradiction

There are also several interesting homologies between Pessoa's artistic practice and his responses to political events of the day. By 1916, the government of then republican prime minister Afonso Costa had entered the war and had become unpopular because of food rationing, inflation, and heavy casualties. In late 1917, Costa's government was overthrown by the military, led by Sidónio Pais, a charismatic figure who imposed a dictatorship. Authoritarian rule was welcomed by many, including Pessoa, who had become disillusioned with parliamentary government, and who saw Pais as a strong leader bringing order to the "desordem múltipla" [multiple disorder] (3:859) of the "Velha República" [Old Republic]. Pais's rule, which Tom Gallagher has called the "first modern republican dictatorship in Europe,"[33] was cut short by an assassination, but it lived on in the form of *sidonismo*—a popular belief that associated the young, energetic leader with the doomed Sebastião. In fact, two years after Pais's death, Pessoa published a long poem entitled "À Memória do Presidente-Rei Sidónio Pais" [To the memory of the President-King Sidónio Pais], in which he portrays Pais as the incarnation of the long-lost king and invokes his return (1:1172–79). He also wrote several fragments for a projected study entitled *O Sentido do Sidonismo* [The meaning of sidonismo].

What exactly were Pessoa's political beliefs, and to what extent do they inform his literary sensibility in general? We can never say exactly, but part of the answer lies in his tendency to view the revolutionary period and its aftermath as a relatively incomplete break with the monarchy, or as a transition toward the nation's ultimate *ressurgimento* [resurgence]. This idea is posited repeatedly in Pessoa's numerous unpublished writings on the republic, which were discovered after his death—in particular in part 2 of his uncompleted book, *Da Ditadura à República: Estudo Sociológico dos Últimos Anos de Monarquia em Portugal e Considerações Post-Revolucionárias* [From the dictatorship to the republic: Sociological study of the last years of the monarchy in Portugal and post-revolutionary considerations]:

> A república actual é a continuação do estado de coisas da monarquia, com simplesmente isto a mais: a abolição do facto que impedia sequer a pensabilidade de melhorar esse estado de coisas . . . O estado de coisas social não muda de momento; começa a exercer-se sobre ele obscuramente a influência de uma outra corrente, purificadora esta, que lentamente vai alterando esse modo-de-ser social. (3:834)

> [The present republic is the continuation of the state of things from the monarchy with simply this addition: the abolishment of the factor that impeded even the thought of bettering that state of things . . . The social state of things does not change at a moment's notice; the influence of another, purifying current begins to exert itself subtly over this social way-of-being, and slowly goes about changing it.]

Pessoa's emphasis on the importance of the past in his political writings is a sign of his continuing sympathy with the views of Pascoaes, who saw the future greatness of Portugal inextricably linked to the past and proclaimed that "O Passado é indestructível" [The Past is indestructible].[34] In a text written between 1914 and 1915, Pessoa wrote: "Uma nação, em qualquer período, é três coisas: 1) uma relação com o passado; 2) uma relação com o presente, nacional e estrangeiro; 3) uma direcção para o futuro" [A nation, in any period, is three things: 1) a relation with the past; 2) a relation with the present, national and foreign; 3) a direction toward the future] (3:595).

Pessoa's attitude toward both society and art is therefore in many ways conservative. Like several other European modernists, he was elitist and outspokenly antidemocratic, as his unfinished political treatise entitled *Oligarquia das Bestas* [Oligarchy of the beasts] makes abundantly clear. He also published an article in defense of the 1926 military takeover that brought an end to the republic and opened the way for Salazar's Estado Novo, a dictatorship that endured until 1974, nearly forty years after Pessoa's death.[35] In important respects, however, Pessoa was highly unconventional, especially in his renunciation of Catholicism and all other forms of organized religion and in his fervent belief in Sebastianism and the mystical practices of anti-Catholic associations like the Masons and Rosicru-cians. In the *Diário de Notícias*, he publicly attacked the Estado Novo's 1935 decree that outlawed all secret associations, and he even wrote a few satirical poems about Salazar and the dictatorship. What makes Pessoa such a fascinating and contradictory writer is this blending of an elite nationalistic sentiment, which favored authoritarian leaders, with certain strains of avant-garde poetics and anticlerical mysticism. (In a biographical note written in 1926, he described himself as a "mystical nationalist"—against communism and socialism and yet absolutely antireactionary [3:1428–9]).

The mixture of national, mystic, folkloric, and modern ideas helps to explain the separate writings produced by Pessoa's heteronyms. As the next chapter will demonstrate, the vast corpus of lyric poems signed by Pessoa "himself" are based on forms and themes associated with medieval or early Renaissance verse; at the same time, these poems are clearly the product of a modern self-consciousness. Meanwhile, the volume *Mensagem* (1934), also signed by Pessoa, has a great deal in common with the major works of European high modernism, especially in its attempt to fuse a classical tradition with a modern sense of disjuncture or montage. Rather like Eliot's *The Waste Land*, it is a "resurgence" of the past into the present. The most overtly nationalistic of Pessoa's writings, it is also the product of a more general or international literary interest in the relations between myth and modernity, cultural continuity and fragmentation.

Ultimately, these powerful contradictions were not manageable within single poems. Pessoa needed the larger universe of the heteronyms to make them play off against one another in truly dynamic fashion. In the last analysis, the heteronyms were overdetermined, the product of many divisions within Pessoa's subjectivity. In important respects, however, they were influenced by cultural and political divisions in the life of the nation as a whole. Hence the four "authors" of Pessoa's major works—the pantheistic Caeiro, the neoclassicist Reis, the modernist Campos, and the slightly alienated romantic known as Pessoa "himself"—function rather like separate historical discourses that maintain an ongoing dialogue. In this way, the past and present intermingle, and history itself is seen as inextricably part of the here and now.

3

The Poetry of Fernando Pessoa

By 1914, Pessoa had developed his system of "heteronymous" poetry.[1] Writings by the four major heteronyms appeared in literary periodicals during his lifetime, although the only book of poems in Portuguese to appear before his death was *Mensagem,* a sequence of short verses on a patriotic or "epic" theme, which was signed by "himself."

In his letter of January 13, 1935, to Adolfo Casais Monteiro, in which he outlined the origins of the heteronyms, Pessoa remarked, "Quando às vezes pensava na ordem de uma futura publicação de obras minhas, nunca um livro do género de *'Mensagem'* figurava em número um" [When at times I thought about the order of a future publication of my works, a book of *Mensagem*'s kind never figured as number one] (2:337). Pessoa considered *Mensagem* to be a "unilateral manifestation" or solitary aspect of a multivoiced oeuvre, and he informed Casais Monteiro that he hoped by year's end to publish a much larger volume containing miscellaneous small poems—a volume that would represent other features of this single poet's personality (2:338). In an earlier letter to João Gaspar Simões (in which he announced a plan to publish *Mensagem* before any other volume because "tem possibilidades de êxito que nenhum dos outros tem" [it has possibilities for success that none of the others has] (2:309), Pessoa proposed the title *Cancioneiro,* or "songbook," for the second book. At that very moment, however, he expressed a certain indifference, remarking that any "equally unexpressive" title would do for what he characterized as a "loose and unclassifiable" body of poetry (2:308). His statement has a disingenuous ring: *Cancioneiro* was the only title he specified (he repeated it twice in the letter), and it tended to reinforce Pessoa's desire to associate his work with the country's oldest and most "authentic" traditions of verse.[2]

The second volume that Pessoa imagined never appeared. However, after his death, editors of his complete works constructed their own version of the *Cancioneiro,* comprising lyric verses of various kinds, ranging from two-line poems and *quadras* [quatrains] to much longer forms. For reasons that are unclear, the editors excluded from this section hundreds of other *quadras* that Pessoa had written between 1907 and 1935 and had placed in a separate envelope in his trunk. Many of these appear in another section of the complete works, entitled *Quadras ao Gosto Popular* [Quatrains in the popular vein].

Together with *Mensagem,* the various shorter poems and lyrics signed by Pessoa create a fairly consistent personality or imaginative world, allowing the author to emerge as a sort of character. One obvious feature of these poems is their tendency to evoke the philosophy and cultural politics of the *saudosistas.* In his lyrics, Pessoa made ample use of *saudade,* the emotional hallmark of *saudosismo,* and he wrote extensively about a traditional, folkloric culture. He composed a number of metaphysical, symbolic, or "esoteric" verses (separated by the editors from the *Cancioneiro*) that seem consistent with the autodidactic, quasi-religious themes of early European modernism.[3] In *Mensagem,* he draws on Sebastianism and its associated prophesies of the Fifth Empire in order to suggest a spiritual/cultural resurgence of Portuguese identity. He was also attracted to the "mystery" that Teixeira de Pascoaes identified as central to the *saudosista* creed, or "a face que a vida não desvendou ainda ao nosso espírito" [the face that life still has not unmasked to our spirit].[4] In both his lyric and epic poems, he frequently uses such words as *enigma, mistério* [mystery], *sombra* [shadow], *sonho* [dream], *Além* [Beyond], *névoa* [fog], and *nevoeiro* [mist] in order to create a mystical or mysterious ambiance.

These poems nevertheless have a paradoxical effect: even though they are attributed to the "real" Pessoa, they are quite impersonal works. The poet called Fernando Pessoa (as distinct from the Pessoa of the letters and critical writings) is a nationalist who is chiefly inspired by two complementary forms of writing associated with Portugal in the Middle Ages and early Renaissance. (Although the miscellaneous lyric poems are sometimes executed in a romantic style, they are clearly inspired by an "anonymous," quasi-folkloric literature that Pessoa celebrated in his *Quadras ao Gosto Popular.*) Thus, on one hand, "Pessoa" writes a kind of epic sequence about Portugal's legendary past and uncertain future; on the other hand, he composes numerous artfully simple songs about life in the open air of the provinces. All of his work depicts a world quite remote from the one in which he actually lived. This work also depends upon a sophisticated modern transformation of earlier models and is the very opposite of an autobiographical or confessional poetry.

Photograph of Pessoa circa 1915.

Mensagem

In 1934, the Salazar government announced a contest for the best volume of nationalistic verse. *Mensagem,* a slim book of forty-four brief poems published that year, won first prize in the category for works under one hundred pages.[5] The competition offered Pessoa the unique opportunity to present himself as the national poet or "Supra-Camões." In an interview that appeared in *Revista Portuguesa* in 1923, he had argued that Camões was too close in time to the events and figures he wrote about in *Os Lusíadas* [The Lusiads] (1572), and that it would be left to a later writer to compose the great epic of this period (3:702–3).[6]

Mensagem is composed of heterogeneous poems that were written over a number of years, and it contains just six hundred lines—longer than Eliot's *The Waste Land* but quite brief in comparison to the approximately eight thousand lines in *Os Lusíadas*. Here it should be noted that one of the nineteenth-century writers Pessoa most admired, Edgar Allan Poe, had criticized the epic poem on the grounds that "true" poetic intensity could not be sustained in a form longer than one hundred lines. The modernists, who were descendants of the nineteenth-century aesthetes, were generally in agreement with this thesis; at every level they attempted to divest poetry of "rhetoric," and they usually substituted imagistic effects for narration.[7] Pessoa himself once declared in English that "[t]he novel having come, we can omit the epic in the poem" (3:56). He much preferred dramatic techniques, giving as an example Tennyson's *Mort d'Arthur,* whose "luminous beauty" he contrasted with the "dull good-writing" of the later and much lengthier *Idylls of the King*. Pessoa avoided "dullness" in *Mensagem* by replacing the traditional *canto* with a series of brief rhymed lyrics of irregular lengths which move back and forth in time, representing different voices or points of view. He may have had a dramatic form in mind when he compiled the volume, as is suggested by the various "soliloquies" spoken by historic figures. Nevertheless, the over-all effect is more like a montage, with individuals and events from different moments juxtaposed in order to suggest an eternal recurrence of Sebastianism, the "nothing that is everything" that Pessoa believed could transform the Portuguese people and their nation into a "Spiritual Empire."

Although it depicts such figures as Ulysses (who supposedly founded the city of Lisbon), *Mensagem* deals chiefly with the fifteenth and sixteenth centuries, the period when the Portuguese colonized areas of Africa, Asia, the Middle East, and South America. This was the era memorialized in *Os Lusíadas,* which describes Vasco da Gama's historic 1498 voyage around the Cape of Good Hope to India. Camões was, of course, born during the period of expansionism and died before its demise. He was a man of action who witnessed some of the events he writes about, and his epic poem is dedicated to King Sebastião, who, in just a few years, would depart for Africa, bringing to a close Portugal's "Golden Age." By contrast, Pessoa is a thoroughly modern figure who has an intense awareness of history as a kind of *textuality*. The events and figures of his poetic sequence are no longer simply past; they are already represented in an official literary masterpiece, and they have been transformed over the centuries into a myth about the rise and fall of a nation that is seeking to return to its former greatness. As a result, Pessoa dispenses with the narrative mode altogether, arranging short poems into a form that seems timeless and virtually actionless. *Os Lusíadas* functions as *Mensagem*'s ghostly intertext, its memory of heroic deeds. *Mensagem* itself is in many ways a static or emblematic volume, filled with religious and mystical symbols—as in the title poem of the third section, "O Encoberto" [The hidden one], which uses cryptic rhetorical questions and Rosicrucian imagery in a style reminiscent of the early Yeats:

> Que símbolo fecundo
> Vem na aurora ansiosa?
> Na Cruz Morta do Mundo
> A Vida, que é a Rosa.
>
> Que símbolo divino
> Traz o dia já visto?
> Na Cruz, que é o Destino,
> A Rosa, que é o Cristo.
>
> Que símbolo final
> Mostra o sol já desperto?
> Na Cruz morta e fatal
> A Rosa do Encoberto. (1:1163)

> [What fecund symbol
> Comes in the anxious dawn?
> On the Dead Cross of the World
> Life, that is the Rose.
>
> What divine symbol
> Brings the day just seen?
> On the Cross, that is Destiny,
> The Rose, that is Christ.
>
> What final symbol
> Shows the sun just awakened?
> On the dead and fatal Cross
> The Rose of the Hidden One.]

The volume as a whole is divided into three parts, whose titles have specific nationalistic implications: "Brasão" refers to the coat of arms that appears on the Portuguese flag; "Mar Português" [Portuguese Sea] symbolizes Portugal's historic eminence as a once-powerful maritime nation; and "O Encoberto" [The hidden one] is an allusion to Sebastião, who, according to popular belief, would return shrouded in mist to save the nation. This arrangement implies a kind of Second Coming, but Pessoa's more important aim is to create a feeling of idealized, transhistorical essence, allowing temporal and spatial oppositions to collapse into paradox. Consider the remarkable opening poem, "O dos Castelos" [Of the castles]:

A Europa jaz, posta nos cotovelos:
De Oriente a Occidente jaz, fitando,
E toldam-lhe românticos cabelos
Olhos gregos, lembrando.

O cotovelo esquerdo é recuado;
O direito é em ângulo disposto.
Aquele diz Itália onde é pousado;
Este diz Inglaterra onde, afastado,
A mão sustenta, em que se apoia o rosto.

Fita com olhar esfíngico e fatal,
O Occidente, futuro do passado.

O rosto com que fita é Portugal. (1:1145)

[Europe reclines, leaning on her elbows:
From East to West she lies, staring,
Romantic tresses over
Greek eyes, remembering.

Her left elbow is drawn back;
The right is at a prone angle.
The former rests upon Italy;
The latter England where, far removed,
It supports the hand on which rests the face.

She stares, with a sphinx-like and fatal gaze,
At the West, future of the past.

The face with which she stares is Portugal.]

Here Portugal is depicted as the sphinx-like "face" of Europe, looking out toward the "future of the past," gazing west in order to return east. Notice, however, that the mystical dissolution of binary oppositions serves a quite historical and ideological purpose, evoking the age of discoveries as well as Pessoa's belief in a Whitmanesque "Atlantic spirit," which will enable Portugal to become the leader of a new European Renaissance.[8] Much the same effect can be seen in "Ulisses" [Ulysses], which begins with a paradoxical comment on the nature of myth: "O mito é o nada que é tudo" [Myth is the nothing that is everything] (1:1146)—an idea that is repeated

in different ways throughout *Mensagem*.[9] By foregrounding such a contradiction, Pessoa is able to seem both a modern skeptic (myth is nothing) and
a true idealist who lives by faith (myth is everything). In one sense, his entire
poetic career is built on similar patterns of disavowal and reassertion: the
heteronyms, for example, suggest that the poet's "self" is nothing more
than an empty signifier or a series of subject positions in language; at the
same time, they imply a transcendent subjectivity or a collective European
"mind."

Other poems in "Brasão" and elsewhere in the volume concern such
historical figures as Viriato, the Lusitanian leader who held off the Roman
invasion of northern Portugal for eight years; Dom Afonso Henriques,
Portugal's first king, who recaptured Lisbon from the Moors in 1147; and
Dom Dinis, one of Portugal's greatest monarchs, who was an accomplished
poet as well as innovator in the areas of agriculture and commerce. Among
these is "D. Sebastião, Rei de Portugal," who speaks in his own voice,
exulting in the "madness" for glory that drove him to his "folly":

Louco, sim, louco porque quis grandeza
Qual a Sorte a não dá.
Não coube em mim minha certeza;
Por isso onde o areal está
Ficou meu ser que houve, não o que há.

Minha loucura, outros que me a tomem
Com o que nela ia.
Sem a loucura que é o homem
Mais que a besta sadia,
Cadáver adiado que procria? (1:1152)

Mad, yes, mad, because I wanted greatness
The sort that Luck doesn't grant.
My certainty didn't fit within me;
Thus, where the sand dune is
Lies my being that was, not that which is.

My madness, let others take it from me
With what it held inside.
Without madness what is man
Except a healthy beast,
A postponed corpse that procreates?]

In addition to this Nietzschean superman who symbolizes the will to power, "Brasão" also includes two women whose patriotism was demonstrated by their procreation of male offspring. Dona Tareja is praised for her "seio augusto" [august breast], which nurtured Portugal's first king; and the English Dona Filipa, whose children included Prince Henry the Navigator, is celebrated as the "humano ventre do Império" [human womb of the Empire].[10]

The twelve poems of "Mar Português" are focused on the "Golden Age" of Portuguese expansion. Among the figures to appear in this section are Prince Henry the Navigator and the voyagers Diogo Cão, Bartolomeu Dias, Fernão de Magalhães, and Vasco da Gama. Here the sequence verges on narrative, especially in "O Mostrengo" [The monster], which alludes to Adamastor, symbol of the terrifying unknown at the end of the world in *Os Lusíadas*. Pessoa describes a winged creature who thrice circles a Portuguese ship while venting its rage:

. . . "Quem é que ousou entrar
Nas minhas cavernas que não desvendo,
Meus tectos negros do fim do mundo?" (1:1156)

. . . ["Who dared to enter
My caverns which I do not disclose,
My black roofs at the end of the world?"]

The Portuguese critic Helder Macedo has noted that while Pessoa sought to outdo *Os Lusíadas,* he actually turned Camões into the great structuring absence of *Mensagem* through this very poem.[11] But in this case Pessoa also reminds us of his debt to the aesthetic movement. "O Mostrengo" was written in 1918; and the dark, forbidding atmosphere of the poem, with its series of exchanges between the birdlike creature and a lone helmsman, resembles nothing so much as Poe's "The Raven," which Pessoa translated in the same year. (Pessoa had originally called the poem "O Morcego" [The bat]—a title more directly evocative of Poe's gothic style.)

The third part of *Mensagem* focuses on the myth of Sebastianism and the utopian commonwealth known as "O Quinto Império" [The Fifth Empire]. Of the many authors who wrote on this subject, Pessoa singled out two for special mention: "O Bandarra," the sixteenth-century cobbler who, prior to Sebastião's demise, composed *trovas* [popular lyrics] about a messianic figure who would usher in the empire; and the seventeenth-century Jesuit priest, António Vieira, whose belief in Bandarra's prophesies inspired his book *Esperanças de Portugal, Quinto Império do Mundo, Primeira e Segunda Vida del-Rei D. João VI* [Hopes for Portugal, fifth empire of the world, first and second life of King D. João VI], which was condemned by the Inquisition. A third, unnamed figure is the subject of an untitled poem which critics have suggested might be a direct statement by Pessoa "himself." This poem begins as if it were a lyrical evocation of *saudade:* "'Screvo meu livro à beira-mágoa'" ["I'm writing my book on the shores of sorrow"]. The poet longs for a messiah, a figure who resembles both Christ and Sebastião, whom he addresses as "Senhor" and "O Encoberto"; and in an intimate appeal bordering on a litany, he implores, "Quando quererás voltar?" [When might you wish to return?] and "Quando virás?" [When will you come?] (1:1165). *Mensagem* then concludes with "O Nevoeiro" [The mist], whose title is an explicit reference to "O Encoberto," who will return shrouded in fog. Here Portugal itself is seen as a spirit covering the earth in a kind of gloom, portending the arrival of a savior. The poem's final line, "É a Hora!" [It's the Hour!] (1:1168), declares the poet's readiness for the fulfillment of the prophecy.[12]

Unlike *Os Lusíadas, Mensagem* treats its historical figures from afar, absorbing them into a Sebastian myth and attempting to exchange a material for a spiritual empire. Pessoa once wrote: "Desejo ser um criador de mitos, que é o mistério mais alto que pode obrar alguém da humanidade" [I want to be a creator of myths, which is the highest mystery that someone can produce of humanity]. But in his modern "epic," Pessoa did not actually create anything new; instead, he drew images from an existent body of ancient lore and legend, fusing them with Sebastianist mysticism. The result is a reformulation of a myth: Portugal becomes a symbolist abstraction and Pessoa its disembodied voice.

The Lyric and Short Poems

Poetry is not a turning loose of emotion, but an escape from emotion; it is not the expression of personality, but an escape from personality. But, of course, only those who have personality and emotions know what it means to want to escape from these things.

T. S. Eliot, "Tradition and the Individual Talent"

The short verses in Portuguese signed by Pessoa derive much of their power from what I described in the previous chapter as a tension between nationalism and modernism. But these poems also manifest a dynamic interplay between two important tendencies within European modernism itself. Borrowing language from T. S. Eliot, we could name these tendencies "tradition and the individual talent," or perhaps "classicism and romanticism." Several of the characteristic figures of high modernity (including T. E. Hulme and Eliot) are associated with the first tendency, which entails a doctrine of impersonality and a severe formal perfectionism; other modern-istic poets (such as Walt Whitman and Hart Crane) exemplify the second tendency, which is associated with emotional effusiveness and con-fessionalism. Pessoa (meaning in this case the man who wrote *all* the poems of the various heteronyms) is situated between the two extremes, but he belongs more in the first camp than in the second. Indeed, the lyric poems signed by Pessoa could be understood as an elaborate formal strategy for holding the personal or confessional at bay, allowing emotion to emerge only when mediated by artistic convention or a fictional persona. Pessoa suggests as much in his famous letter to Casais Monteiro:

> Referi-me, como viu, ao Fernando Pessoa só. Não penso nada do Caeiro, do Ricardo Reis ou do Álvaro de Campos. Nada disso poderei fazer, no sentido de publicar, excepto quando . . . me for dado o Prémio Nobel. E contudo—penso-o com tristeza—pus no Caeiro todo o meu poder de despersonalização dramática, pus em Ricardo Reis toda a minha disciplina mental, vestida da música que lhe é própria, pus em Álvaro de Campos toda a emoção que não dou nem a mim nem à vida. Pensar, meu querido Casais Monteiro, que todos estes têm que ser, na prática da publicação, preteridos pelo Fernando Pessoa, impuro e simples! (2:338)

> [As you see, I referred only to Fernando Pessoa. I'm not thinking any-thing about Caeiro, Ricardo Reis or Álvaro de Campos. Nothing of this will I be able to do, in the sense of publication, except when . . . the Nobel Prize is given to me. And nevertheless—I think of it with sadness—I put in Caeiro all my power of dramatic depersonalization, I put in Ricardo Reis all my mental discipline, dressed in the music that is appropriate to him, I put in Álvaro de Campos all the emotion that I give neither to myself nor to life. To think, my dear Casais Monteiro, that for the practical purpose of publication, these three have to be passed over for Fernando Pessoa, impure and artless!]

Interestingly, the Whitmanesque persona Álvaro de Campos is the only "emotional" poet mentioned in this passage, and Pessoa wistfully remarks that Campos represents a tendency that "I give neither to myself nor to life." Caeiro and Reis are characterized by extreme forms of "depersonal-ization" and "mental discipline," whereas Fernando Pessoa "himself" seems to be situated somewhere in the "impure and artless" middle. As a result, the heteronym known as Pessoa serves to dramatize the split be-tween reason and feeling, between consciousness and direct sensation.

One way in which Pessoa keeps excessively personal or emotional material at bay is through the use of highly traditional verse forms, especially the Portuguese *quadra,* which has been given insufficient attention in commentaries on his work. In the early 1960s, Georg Lind discovered that Pessoa had spent the last two years of his life writing hundreds of these "popular" verses. Yet, even Lind, who wrote a preface to the first edition of *Quadras ao Gosto Popular,* seems to have regarded them as relatively minor and unsymptomatic: "Quem podia supor que um espírito tão cerebral e especulativo condescendesse em cultivar um género tão simples e popular" [Who could suppose that such a cerebral and speculative spirit *would condescend* (my emphasis) to cultivating such a simple and popular genre].[13] In my own view, Pessoa's fondness for the *quadras* is far from surprising. Such poems are consistent with the essentially nationalistic character of the work he attributed to "himself," and they imply a particular attitude toward history. Again and again, the author named Pessoa points back nostalgically to a predemocratic culture, linking the Portuguese national identity with an imaginary yet compellingly pristine view of the countryside.

At bottom, of course, the folkloricism and simplicity of the *quadras* are mere literary conceits. Notice the different and far more wryly confessional tone in "Alentejo Seen from a Train," a piece of light verse Pessoa wrote in English in 1907, during his trip to purchase a printing press in the small town of Portalegre:

> Nothing with nothing around it
> And a few trees in between
> None of which very clearly green,
> Where no river or flower pays a visit.
> If there be a hell, I've found it,
> For if it ain't here, where the Devil is it? (2:128)[14]

When forced to live in the provinces, Pessoa reacted with a typical cosmopolitan's dismay. As long as the countryside could be viewed through the lens of a literary pastoralism or primitivism, however, it took on a more appealing look. A myth of the countryside became important to Pessoa as an expression of his politics. For all his attraction to modernism, he did not want to forsake the idea that he was fundamentally a *Portuguese* poet, who was helping to preserve what he regarded as traditional customs.

Pessoa approached the *quadra* with the same attitudes that characterized his early "mote e glosa": in keeping with tradition, all his later *quadras* as well as many of those in the *Cancioneiro* are written in the *redondilha* meter, and most subscribe to the conventional *abcb* rhyme pattern. In terms of subject matter, they are subtle reworkings of topoi long associated with folk verse; among the more prominent motifs are love, nature, music, agrarian life, and *saudade*. The scholar Jacinto do Prado Coelho was the first to comment on the first of these motifs: "[N]ão se tem lamentado na obra de Fernando Pessoa a quase total ausência da mulher e do amor? Pois bem: aqui, nas quadras 'populares', ele surge principalmente como poeta do amor" [Hasn't the almost total absence of women and love been lamented in the work of Fernando Pessoa? Very well; here, in the "popular" *quadras*, he emerges principally as a poet of love].[15] It is important to note, however, that the object of the poet's attention is not an actual figure of his experience but the quintessential peasant girl of the "cancioneiro popular," a literary convention as stylized and remote as the medieval "lady of the court."[16] Pessoa was also adept at investing conventional images with a sort of deflating, antiromantic wit. In the example below, he plays with the familiar motif of the woman's ring, traditionally a symbol of love, transforming it into a sign of the woman's infidelity:

Quem te deu aquele anel
Que ainda ontem não tinhas?
Como tu foste infiel
A certas ideias minhas! (1:541)

[Who gave you that ring
That even yesterday you didn't have?
How you were unfaithful
To certain ideas of mine!]

True, the love poems by Pessoa are frequently quite sensuous:

Loura dos olhos dormentes
Que são azuis e amarelos,
Se as minhas mãos fossem pentes,
Penteavam-te os cabelos. (1:532)

[Blond with dreamy eyes
That are blue and yellow,
If my hands were combs,
They would comb your tresses.]

In typical Pessoan fashion, however, there is no physical contact between the poet and the woman—merely the suggestion of a love rendered impossible by the subjunctive clause. The distance implied here is in keeping with a comment by Pessoa in English that "the best sort of love poetry is generally written about an abstract woman" (3:63).

Another kind of distancing can be seen in one of the most widely admired of Pessoa's lyric poems, "Ela canta, pobre ceifeira" [She sings, poor reaper], which was first published in the literary review *Athena* in 1924:

Ela canta, pobre ceifeira,
Julgando-se feliz talvez;
Canta, e ceifa, e a sua voz, cheia
De alegre e anónima viuvez,

Ondula como um canto de ave
No ar limpo como um limiar,
E há curvas no enredo suave
Do som que ela tem a cantar.

Ouvi-la alegra e entristece,
Na sua voz há o campo e a lida,
E canta como se tivesse
Mais razões p'ra cantar que a vida.

Ah, canta, canta sem razão!
O que em mim sente 'stá pensando.
Derrama no meu coração
A tua incerta voz ondeando!

Ah, poder ser tu, sendo eu!
Ter a tua alegre inconsciência,
E a consciência disso! Ó céu!
Ó campo! Ó canção! A ciência

Pesa tanto e a vida é tão breve!
Entrai por mim dentro! Tornai
Minha alma a vossa sombra leve!
Depois, levando-me, passai! (1:187–88)

[She sings, poor reaper,
Thinking herself happy perhaps;
She sings and she reaps and her voice, full
Of joyful and anonymous widowhood,

Quavers like the song of a bird
Limpid as a threshold in the air,

And there are curves in the gentle story
Of the song that she has to sing.

To hear her delights and saddens,
In her voice there is the field and labor,
And she sings as if she had
More reasons to sing than life itself.

Ah, sing, sing without reason!
What in me feels is thinking.
Pour into my heart
Your uncertain, quavering voice!

Ah, to be able to be you, being me!
To have your joyful unconsciousness,
And the consciousness of it! Oh heaven!
Oh field! Oh song! Science

Weighs so much and life is so brief!
Enter into me! Turn
My soul into your lofty shadow!
Then, carrying me away, pass on!]

In this instance, a kind of passion or un-self conscious emotion is observed from a distance and is mediated through poetic convention or imitation. "Ela canta, pobre ceifeira" has been treated by critics Peter Rickard and Bernard McGuirk, among others,[17] as a specific imitation of Wordsworth's "The Solitary Reaper" (1807). In making this connection, however, critics have overlooked or deemphasized the equally important Portuguese sources of the poem, especially the early, proverbial form of the *quadra* in the "cancioneiro popular." "Ela canta, pobre ceifeira" was completed in 1914—the year in which Pessoa published a glowing tribute to the *quadra* in the anthology *Missal de Trovas* [Missal of songs]. That same year he had also translated a volume of Portuguese proverbs into English.[18] In a recent analysis of the *Cancioneiro Popular Português*, Maria Nunes emphasizes the ideological significance of the proverbial tradition. She contends that such mottoes as "trabalha e cria, terás alegria" [work and (pro)create, and you'll have joy], were influential in creating a kind of verse that celebrated the humblest of laborers and the sense of fulfillment they presumably derived from their daily chores. According to Nunes, the figures that most commonly appeared in *quadras* were "viscerally Portuguese" types, such as the shepherd, the fisherman, and the reaper, who were also representative of the different regions in Portugal. She further remarks that women were prominent figures in the songs and that the voice in the poem is often a woman's:

> Vida de trabalho, ao ar livre, expostas às inclemências do tempo, tanto ao calor como ao frio, passam diante de nós a ["]ceifeira que anda[s] à calma / No campo a ceifar o trigo," a mondadeira, a sachadeira, a lavadeira: "Cada qual tem seu ofício, / Eu também sou lavadeira,"—a leiteira que declara: "Sou leiteira, vendo leite, / Também vendo requeijão."

> [Life of work in the open air, exposed to the inclemencies of weather, to the heat as well as to the cold, before us passes the "reaper, who walks calmly / Harvesting the wheat in the field," the weeder, the hoer, the washerwoman: "Every one has their own job, / I too am a washerwoman,"—the milkwoman, who declares: "I'm a milkwoman, I sell milk, / I also sell curd cheese."[19]

The lines quoted by Nunes on the reaper are from a *quadra* from the Alentejo, a region of Portugal where wheat fields and reapers abound. They are typical of a genre of folk verse that described even the most debilitating forms of labor, such as sowing and reaping, in terms of the worker's tranquil if not happy disposition.[20] This tradition ultimately found its way into the works of the Portuguese romantics, who were drawn to the "simplicity" and "local color." In 1913, the *saudosista* Teixeira de Pascoaes offered a similarly pastoral vision in his essay, "O Génio Português na sua Expressão Filosófica, Poética e Religiosa" [The Portuguese genius in its philosophical, poetic, and religious expression]: "O nosso Povo do campo e da beira-mar conserva ainda aceso, dentro de si, qual sagrado lume inviolável, o génio puro da Raça. Louvemos o feliz isolamento em que tem vivido, longes dos grandes centros onde tudo se adultera: o pão do corpo e do espírito" [Our People of the countryside and coast still keep burning within themselves such an inviolable sacred light, the pure genius of the Race. Let us praise the happy isolation in which they have lived, far from the great centers where everything is adulterated: the bread of the body and spirit].[21]

Pessoa's "Ela canta, pobre ceifeira" therefore derives from a type of European pastoralism which, in Portugal alone, can be dated back to the earliest songs and adages of "o povo" [the people]. Indeed, the image of the reaper was so familiar by the time the poem was written that the initial *quadra* has the quality of a *mote* whose theme is "glossed" in the subsequent two stanzas. In this regard, it should be noted that Pessoa's reaper is treated somewhat differently from the stereotypes of the romantics and *fin-de-siècle* poets. The phrases "pobre ceifeira" [*poor* reaper] and "Julgando-se feliz talvez" [*Believing* herself to be happy *perhaps*] (my emphasis) subtly interject a note of uncertainty about whether the reaper is truly content.[22] Her "voz incerta canta como se tivesse / Mais razões p'ra cantar que a vida" [*uncertain* voice sings *as if* she had / More reasons to sing than life itself (my emphasis)].

The theme of uncertainty makes the comparison between "Ela canta, pobre ceifeira" and Wordsworth's "Solitary Reaper" especially revealing. As Peter Rickard has observed:

> ["Ela canta"] was certainly inspired by Wordsworth's "The Reaper," and contains verbal reminiscences of it: yet it also contains the typically Pessoan idea of something lacking, and the longing for the impossible. Wordsworth wants to know what the solitary reaper is singing about: for Pessoa, this is a matter of indifference. He wants to be the singer *and yet himself* at the same time. He wants to be, like the reaper, "blithely unaware," as he puts it, but at the same time aware that he is blithely unaware. And the appeal to sky, field, and song with which the Portuguese poem ends, is quite lacking in Wordsworth.[23]

McGuirk also gives special attention to Pessoa's "thinking and feeling" speaker, and contrasts him with the Wordsworthian "I," who is wholly caught up in the emotion of the song. Clearly Pessoa's singing reaper is a pretext for a commentary on the poet, whose "divided" self becomes the primary focus. And yet ironically, despite the poet's relative alienation, "Ela canta, pobre ceifeira" is as graceful and beautiful as the reaper's song. The effect has something in common with Wallace Stevens's "The Idea of Order at Key West" (1934), in which a distant singer brings aesthetic "order" to the perceptions of two observers. In Pessoa's poem, the flourish of exclamations in the final stanzas creates a feeling of uninhibited celebration which overshadows the element of sorrow. Like the reaper's melody, the poem both "saddens and delights" through its contrasting images of a self in conflict and the poetic exuberance of the lyrics "sung."

Pessoa once wrote in English, "[w]hen an age aches for something new (if ages ever ache), it wants something old" (3:48). In the case of the lyric poetry by "himself," he focused on themes and forms specific to anonymous Portuguese oral and literary traditions, creating in the process his own distinct *Cancioneiro*, whose most salient feature is its mixture of nostalgia and vague longing. He was intent upon forging something "startling and new," convinced that "[t]he real novelty that endures is the one that has taken up all the threads of tradition and weaved them again into a pattern that tradition could not weave them into" (3:59). What makes his work distinctive is his inability or refusal to experience what Kant described as the *Ding an sich*. He was always guarded when it came to the direct experience of the physical world or to the direct expression of emotion. In another context, again writing in English, he remarked: "Three sorts of emotions produce great poetry—strong but quick emotions, seized upon for art as soon as they have passed, but not before they have passed; strong and deep emotions in their remembrance a long time after; and false emotions, that is to say, emotions felt in the intellect. Not insincerity, yet a translated sincerity, is the basis of all art" (3:63).

To a certain extent, Pessoa's preoccupation with *degrees* of emotion, be they "strong but quick," "strong and deep in their remembrance," or utterly "false," manifests itself in one form or another in nearly everything he wrote. His typology of sentiment gives primacy to the romantic ideal of spontaneity (for example, love), but his lyrics are not spontaneous poems. In "Ela canta, pobre ceifeira," the "pure" emotion of the reaper is contrasted with the poet's "feeling/thinking" self. Here as elsewhere, Pessoa suggests that it is not enough to feel; the poet must be conscious of feelings and, like a "great general," keep them at bay no matter the price in order to carry out the strategy and "win [the] battle" (3:63).

As Georg Lind notes, Pessoa's attitude toward art and emotion is similar to that of T. S. Eliot, who proclaimed in "Tradition and the Individual Talent," that "[t]he emotion of art is impersonal."[24] In fact, Pessoa anticipated Eliot's pronouncement in two long fragments—one in Portuguese and the other in English—written in 1916. In Portuguese, Pessoa wrote: "Só o que se pensa é que se pode comunicar aos outros. O que se sente não se pode comunicar" [One can communicate to others only that which one thinks. One cannot communicate what one feels] (3:190). In the more detailed English fragment, addressed "to an English editor," he summarized the central attitudes of the *sensacionismo* movement in the following way:

1. The only reality in life is sensation. The only reality in art is consciousness of the sensation.

2. . . . Whatever love, joy, pain, may be in life, in art they are only sensations; in themselves they are worthless to art . . .

3. Art, fully defined, is the harmonic expression of our consciousness of sensations; that is to say, our sensations must be so expressed that

they *create an object which will be a sensation to others.* Art is not, as Bacon said, "man added to Nature"; it is sensation multiplied by consciousness—multiplied, be it well noted. (3:193–94)

Pessoa concluded his "letter" with what he regarded as the three principles of art:

1) every sensation should be expressed to the full, that is, the consciousness of every sensation should be sifted to the bottom; 2) the sensation should be so expressed that it has the possibility of evoking—as a halo round a definite central presentation—the greatest possible number of other sensations; 3) the whole thus produced should have the greatest possible resemblance to an organised being, because that is the condition of vitality. I call these three principles 1) that of Sensation, 2) that of Suggestion, 3) that of Construction. This last, the great principle of the Greeks—whose great philosopher did indeed hold the poem to be "an animal"—has had very careless handling at modern hands. Romanticism has indisciplined the capacity of constructing which, at least, low classicism had. (3:194)

Pessoa also elaborated his thoughts on the problematic relation between art and emotion in several of his poems. Consider "A lavadeira no tanque" [The washerwoman at the tub], another of his speculations on a "viscerally Portuguese type." Although the washerwoman is portrayed happily singing as she beats clothes against a rock, the poet interjects a note of uncertainty about her apparent happiness: "Canta porque canta e é triste / Porque canta porque existe; / Por isso é alegre também" [She sings because she sings and is sad / Because she sings because she exists; / Therefore she's also happy] (1:366). The poem then goes on to offer a relatively explicit commentary on emotion and the creative process:

Ora se eu alguma vez
Pudesse fazer nos versos
O que a essa roupa ela fez,
Eu perderia talvez
Os meus destinos diversos.

Há uma grande unidade
Em, sem pensar nem razão,
E até cantando a metade,
Bater roupa em realidade . . .
Quem me lava o coração? (1:366)

[Now if some time I
Could do in verse
What she did to those clothes,
I would perhaps lose
My diverse destinies.

There's a great unity
In, without thinking or reason,
And even singing half,
Beating clothes in reality . . .
Who'll wash my heart for me?]

The subjective "unity" or pure emotion symbolized by the washerwoman's song is something the speaker of the poem can experience only second-hand; he is forever destined to be conscious of what he feels—a condition that leads him to "diverse destinies" (an interesting allusion to the heteronyms and their distinct personalities). As in "Ela canta, pobre ceifeira," the poem achieves its ideal emotionalism by a process Pessoa himself described as "creat[ing] an object which will be a sensation to others."

The ostensibly simple verses of the *Cancioneiro* are filled with references to the poet's inability to express himself directly—a condition that sometimes verges on angst or ennui. In one of the earliest of these poems, "Estado de Alma" [State of the soul] (1910), he claims that he lives "Sem dores nem alegrias, / Mas só em monotonias / De mágoa incompreendida . . ." [Without pain or happiness, / But only in monotonies / Of sorrow misunderstood . . .] (1:159); and in "Tédio" [Tedium], written that same year, he remarks: "Não vivo, mal vegeto, duro apenas, / Vazio dos sentidos porque existo; / . . . E o meu mal é ser (alheio Cristo) / . . . Completamente consciente disto" [I don't live, I barely vegetate, I merely endure, / Empty of feelings because I exist; / . . . And my fate is to be (distanced from Christ) / . . . Completely conscious of this] (1:160). Nine years later, in the poem "Vendaval" [Gale], he returns to the same theme, except that what was earlier the "sorrow" or "tedium" of consciousness is now described as a never-ending nightmare: "Horror de ser sempre com vida a consciência! / Horror de sentir a alma sempre a pensar!" [Horror of always being conscious of life! / Horror of feeling the soul always thinking!] (1:200).

In many of the lyrics, the poet expresses his romantic desire to be free of the burden of inhibiting consciousness, which denies him the apparent tranquillity of the reaper or washerwoman. He wants to belong to "um país / Onde ser feliz consiste / Apenas em ser feliz" [a country / Where being happy consists / Simply in being happy] (1:158). This freedom from thought is evoked through various motifs: the soft flight of a bird, the blue of the sky, and the curve in the horizon—all these things suggest the pure grace or *sossego* [calm] to which the poet aspires and which his "inútil consciência" [futile consciousness] (1:220) repeatedly denies him.

Dreams, sleep, and childhood memories, like the songs of the reaper and the washerwoman, momentarily relieve the poet of tedium. Some critics have regarded these themes, together with Pessoa's use of *saudade,* as an expression of his desire to give up the burdensome consciousness of the present and seek refuge in the past. But Pessoa was not a simple escapist; like Teixeira de Pascoaes, for whom *saudade* represented the "nova claridade" [new clarity], his interest in the "sombra do Passado" [the shadow of the Past] was founded on its connection with "a luz do Futuro" [the light of the Future].[25] Pessoa makes this point very clearly in another passage he wrote in English on the sensationist writers:

> But we do not fall into the narrowness of regionalist movements and such like; we must not be confounded with things like the *"Celtic Revival"* or any Yeats fairynonsense. We are not Portuguese writing for Portuguese; we leave that to journalists and political leader-writers. We are Portuguese writing for Europe, for all civilisation . . .
>
> We work away from Camões, from all the tedious nonsenses of Portuguese tradition, towards the Future. (3:187)

Here we can see the relation between Pessoa's mystic nationalism and his self-conscious emotionalism. At both levels, he is a poet who tries to create a sense of newness rising out of a past remembered or observed at a certain remove. In 1920, he writes about "A lembrada canção, / Amor, renova, agora" [The song recalled, / Love, renew, now] (1:201), and, ten years later, he elaborates on the theme:

No fundo do pensamento
Tenho por sono um cantar,
Um cantar velado e lento,
Sem palavras a falar.

Se eu o pudesse tornar
Em palavras de dizer
Todos haviam de achar
O que ele está a esconder.

Todos haviam de ter
No fundo do pensamento

A novidade de haver
Um cantar velado e lento.

E cada um, desatento
Da vida que tem que achar,
Teria o contentamento
De ouvir esse meu cantar. (1:310)

[In the depth of thought
I have for sleep a song,
A veiled, slow song,
Without words.

If I could turn it
Into words
Everyone would be obliged to find
What it is hiding.

Everyone would be obliged to have
In the depth of their thoughts
The novelty of experiencing
A veiled, slow song.

And each, heedless
Of the life that one has to find,
Would have the contentment
Of hearing this my song.]

In order to tease emotion or a "hidden song" into being, Pessoa argued that the poet should *dramatize* feeling in art—an act which he described as "forgery" or "a notação nítida de uma impressão falsa" [the clear notation of a false impression] (3:29). One of his most celebrated poems takes as its theme the art of "misrepresentation." Its title, "Autopsicografia," derived from the Portuguese *psicografia,* refers to the occult practice of writing through the suggestion or action of a spirit medium:

O poeta é um fingidor.
Finge tão completamente
Que chega a fingir que é dor
A dor que deveras sente.

E os que lêem o que escreve,
Na dor lida sentem bem,
Não as duas que ele teve,

Mas só a que eles não têm.

E assim nas calhas de roda
Gira, a entreter a razão,
Esse comboio de corda
Que se chama o coração. (1:314)

[The poet is a pretender.
He pretends so completely
That he ends up pretending that it's pain
The pain that he truly feels.

And those who read what he writes,
Feel good in reading his pain,
Not the two pains that he had,
Just the one they don't feel.

And so on the tracks
It goes round and round, giving entertainment to reason,
This toy train drawn by a cord,
Known as the heart.]

In this poignant series of *quadras,* Pessoa makes the poet such a master of intellectualizing or feigning that even he cannot tell where pretense leaves off and feeling begins. Artifice and true feeling, pain and pleasure, the reader and the writer—these oppositions become confounded, like the intertwined surfaces of a Möbius strip.

Written in 1931 and published a year later in the literary review *Presença,* "Autopsicografia" is considered Pessoa's ultimate statement on the poetic process. But as early as 1911, in a poem entitled "Análise" [Analysis], we find him clearly enunciating the theme of "translated sincerity":

Tão abstracta é a ideia do teu ser
Que me vem de te olhar, que, ao entreter
Os meus olhos nos teus, perco-os de vista,
E nada fica em meu olhar, e dista
Teu corpo do meu ver tão longemente,
E a ideia do teu ser fica tão rente
Ao meu pensar olhar-te, e ao saber-me
Sabendo que tu és, que, só por ter-me
Consciente de ti, nem a mim sinto.
E assim, neste ignorar-me a ver-te, minto
A ilusão da sensação, e sonho,

Não te vendo, nem vendo, nem sabendo
Que te vejo, ou sequer que sou, risonho
Do interior crepúsculo tristonho
Em que sinto que sonho o que me sinto sendo.
     Do sonho e pouco da vida. (1:162)

[The idea of your being is so abstract to me
That when I look at you and entertain
My eyes with yours, I lose sight of you,
And nothing remains in my gaze, and
Your body moves so far from my sight,
Yet the idea of you is so close
To my intent to look at you, and just knowing
That you are, just by being
Conscious of you, I no longer feel myself.
And thus, by being unaware of seeing you, I feign
The illusion of sensation, and I dream,
Not seeing you, nor seeing, nor knowing
That I see you, or even that I am, smiling
From an inner blue twilight
In which I feel that I dream that which I feel myself being.
     From the dream and little of life.]

"Análise" is one of Pessoa's earliest comments on the paradoxical and deceptive practice of his "own" poetry. Significantly, it is both a poem about love (addressed to an abstract woman) and a poem about the act of writing. It is more free-form and verbose than the vast majority of poems in the *Cancioneiro*, but it is nonetheless an extraordinary attempt to reveal the underlying emotional structure of what Pessoa once referred to as "artistic lying." Perhaps Pessoa could be direct, truthful, and self-revealing only when he was describing the process of art itself.

Pessoa frequently used the "confessional" language of "Autopsicografia" to describe his life as a writer. In 1933, he published "Isto" [This], which begins:

Dizem que finjo ou minto
Tudo que escrevo. Não.
Eu simplesmente sinto
Com a imaginação.
Não uso o coração. (1:352)

[They say that I pretend or lie about
Everything that I write. No.
I simply feel
With my imagination.
I don't use my heart.]

The poem ends somewhat irreverently and impatiently with the exclamation: "Sentir? Sinta quem lê!" [Feel? Let whomever reads feel!].

Rejecting the autobiographical poetry of the romantics, Pessoa spent the last two years of his life composing hundreds of impersonal *quadras* inspired by the verse of the folk. But among these gay and often witty poems about peasant girls, flowered windows, and country life, we also find occasional poems about the act of writing—another popular *quadra* motif, in which the word *pena* is employed for its double meaning of "pen" and "pain." In typical fashion, Pessoa calls attention to the deceptiveness of the pain/pen:

Tenho uma pena que escreve
Aquilo que eu sempre sinta.
Se é mentira, escreve leve.
Se é verdade, não tem tinta. (1:547)

[I have a pen that writes
That which I always feel.
If it's false, it writes light.
If it's true, it has no ink.]

Using the language of this *quadra*, we might describe Pessoa's *Cancioneiro* as "light" or relatively pleasurable verse that depicts something removed, already written, and "false." In a larger sense, all the poetry I have been describing in the foregoing section operates by a similar principle of feigned or dramatized passions. Even though he signed poems as "himself," Pessoa never writes directly from the heart, because to do so would be to lose the necessary distance between his emotions and his craft—in other words, to run out of ink.

4

The Poetry of Alberto Caeiro

Over the years, numerous theories have been put forth about the motives for Pessoa's creation of the heteronyms. Some critics have attributed authors such as Caeiro, Reis, and Campos to the influence of Pessoa's friend Mário de Sá-Carneiro, whose poems and stories frequently turned on the idea of a split within the self. Harold Bloom has viewed Caeiro and Campos in terms of Pessoa's close reading of Whitman, which resulted in a desire to distinguish what the American poet termed the "me myself" and "the real me," or the spiritual and fleshly aspects of humanity.[1] António Quadros and Dalila Pereira da Costa regard the heteronyms as symptoms of a historical period when the notion of the unified self was being called into question by philosophy and psychoanalysis. Mário de Saraiva has gone further along these lines, suggesting that the heteronyms were the result of Pessoa's own schizophrenic personality. For his part, Pessoa himself claimed to have a certain interest in "Freudismo," stating in his typically ironic way that it was a theory "imperfeito, estreito e utilíssimo" [imperfect, narrow, and very useful] (2:298). At one point, he wrote to Adolfo Casais Monteiro about the connection between the heteronyms and a self-diagnosed "histero-neurastenia": "Se eu fosse mulher—na mulher os fenómenos histéricos rompem em ataques e coisas parecidas—cada poema de Álvaro de Campos (o mais histericamente histérico de mim) seria um alarme para a vizinhança. Mas sou homem—e nos homens a histeria assume principalmente aspectos mentais; assim tudo acaba em silêncio e poesia." [If I were a woman—in women hysterical phenomena appear as attacks and the like—each poem by Álvaro de Campos (the most hysterically hysterical part of me) would set off an alarm in the neighborhood. But I'm a man—and in men hysteria assumes primarily mental aspects; thus everything ends in silence and poetry] (2:339).

In one of several prefaces that he drafted for the projected volume en-

titled *Ficções do Interlúdio* [Fictions of the interlude], which would include selections by Caeiro, Reis, and Campos, Pessoa declares that he
does not know whether the heteronyms are the product of a *privilégio*
[privilege] or a *doença* [sickness] (2:1019). Later in the preface, he raises
the possibility that they resulted from "uma forma de histeria" [a kind of
hysteria] or "a chamada dissociação da personalidade" [the so-called
dissociation of personality] (2:1020). Elsewhere, however, he rejects psychological explanations in favor of a straightforward doctrine of aesthetic impersonality:

> Suponhamos que um supremo despersonalizado, como Shakespeare,
> em vez de criar o personagem de Hamlet como parte de um drama, o
> criava como simples personagem, sem drama. Teria escrito, por assim
> dizer, um drama de uma só personagem, um monó-logo prolongado e
> analítico. Não seria legítimo ir buscar a esse personagem uma definição
> dos sentimentos e dos pensamentos de Shakespeare, a não ser que o
> personagem fosse falhado, porque o mau dramaturgo é o que se revela.

> Por qualquer motivo temperamental que me não proponho analisar,
> nem importa que analise, construí dentro de mim várias personagens
> distintas entre si e de mim, personagens essas a que atribuí poemas
> vários que não são como eu, nos meus sentimentos e ideias, os escre-
> veria.

> Assim têm estes poemas de Caeiro, os de Ricardo Reis e os de Álvaro
> de Campos que ser considerados. Não há que buscar em quaisquer
> deles ideias ou sentimentos meus, pois muitos deles exprimem ideias
> que não aceito, sentimentos que nunca tive. Há simplesmente que os ler
> como estão, que é aliás como se deve ler.

> . . . Negar-me o direito de fazer isto seria o mesmo que negar a
> Shakespeare o direito de dar expressão à alma de Lady Macbeth, com
> o fundamento de que ele, poeta, nem era mulher, nem, que se saiba,
> histero-epiléptico, ou de lhe atribuir uma tendência alucinatória e uma
> ambição que não recua perante o crime. Se assim é das personagens
> fictícias de um drama, é igualmente lícito das personagens fictícias sem
> drama, pois que é lícito porque elas são fictícias e não porque estão
> num drama. (1:712–13)

[Let's suppose that a supremely depersonalized author, like
Shakespeare, instead of creating the character Hamlet as part of a

drama, created him as a simple character without a drama. In other words, he would have written a drama with only one character and a prolonged and analytic monologue. It wouldn't be right to go looking to this character for a definition of the feelings and thoughts of Shakespeare, unless the idea of the character were flawed, and then the bad playwright is the one revealing himself.

For temperamental reasons that I do not propose to analyze, nor is it important that I analyze, I constructed within me various characters distinct among themselves and from me—characters to whom I attributed various poems that, in terms of feelings and ideas, are not like those that I would write.

Here then are poems by Caeiro, Reis, and Álvaro de Campos for consideration. There is no reason to seek in any of them ideas or feeling that belong to me, for many of them express ideas that I do not accept, feelings that I never had. They are simply to be read as they are, which is how they should be read.

. . . To deny me the right to do this would be like denying Shakespeare the right to give expression to the soul of Lady Macbeth, based on the fact that he, the poet, was neither a woman nor, that we know, a hystero-epileptic, or to attribute to him some hallucinatory tendency and ambition that doesn't flinch before the crime. If this is true in the case of fictitious characters in a drama, it's equally true of fictitious characters outside a drama, for the nature of the characters derives from their fictitiousness, not from the fact that they appear in a drama.]

As these remarks suggest, Pessoa was quite similar to his modernist contemporaries in England, who were attempting to make poetry more dramatic and dispassionate, more about "showing" than "telling," more charged with what Keats called "negative capability." Based on his comments at the time, he seemed to enjoy carrying the process of impersonation to extremes, creating different fictional and poetic selves who had a life of their own. In a letter to Cortes-Rodrigues in 1914, he tells his friend about a joke that the poet Alfredo Pedro Guisado played on their friend António Ferro (who knew nothing of the heteronyms at the time) in order to convince him of the existence of Alberto Caeiro:

O Guisado encontrou o Ferro acompanhado de um amigo, caixeiro-viajante, aliás. E começou a falar no Caeiro, como tendo-lhe sido apresentado, e tendo trocado duas palavras apenas com ele. "Se

calhar é qualquer lepidóptero" disse o Ferro. "Nunca ouvi falar nele
. . ." E, de repente, soa, inesperada, a voz do caixeiro-viajante: *"Eu já
ouvi falar nesse poeta, e até me parece que já li algures uns versos
dele."* . . . Para o caso de tirar todas as possíveis suspeitas futuras ao
Ferro não se podia exigir melhor. O Guisado ia ficando doente de riso
reprimido, mas conseguiu continuar a ouvir. E não voltou ao assunto,
visto o caixeiro-viajante ter feito tudo o que era necessário. (2:169)

[Guisado met up with Ferro, who was accompanied by a friend, who
was a traveling salesman. And Gusiado started talking about Caeiro,
about having been introduced to him and their having exchanged a
few words. "I'll bet he's some fly-brained fellow," said Ferro. "I never
even heard of him . . . " Suddenly and unexpectedly, the traveling
salesman piped up: *"I've heard of this poet and it even seems to me
that I've read some of his verses."* . . . One couldn't have asked for
anything better to allay any possible future doubt Ferro might have.
Guisado nearly got sick from holding back his laughter, but he managed to go on listening. He never broached the subject again because
the salesman had done everything that was necessary.]

Pessoa seems never to have tired of games of impersonation such as the
ones that filled the pages of his childhood newspapers. But the heteronyms
were not simply a game; they were a highly intellectualized "construction"
that occupied his entire adult life. One of their important functions was to
enable him to exhibit mastery over a range of styles and traditions and to
experiment with different aesthetic positions. In this regard, it is important
to emphasize that while his heteronyms can be classified as "pagan," "neoclassic," "romantic," and "modernist," they are all *contemporary;* they
have historical predecessors, but they represent artistic styles or techniques
that Pessoa believed were relevant to twentieth-century Portugal. When in
1919 T. S. Eliot wrote about the need of the poet to "procure the consciousness of the past," to "develop this consciousness throughout his career,"
and to undergo "a continual self-sacrifice, a continual extinction of personality," Pessoa had already created the heteronyms—including Pessoa "himself"—whose works reflect that "fusion of past elements" which only a
writer with a "historical sense" was able to achieve.[2] For Pessoa, "making
it new" involved a process of rethinking past styles and exploring their
relevance for his own day.

According to Pessoa's 1935 letter to Casais Monteiro, the first heteronym to issue forth in 1914 was Alberto Caeiro. Pessoa's account of this
event is highly dramatic and not to be taken literally: standing at a tall chest

of drawers, and "numa espécie de êxtase cuja natureza não conseguirei definir" [in a kind of ecstasy whose nature I can't define] (2:341), he supposedly dashed off some thirty poems that would form the body of the collection entitled O *Guardador de Rebanhos* [*The Keeper of Sheep*].

As with all his subsequent creations, he gave the new poet a biography and a physical description. In the letter to Casais Monteiro, Pessoa claims that Alberto Caeiro was born in Lisbon in 1889 (one year after Pessoa's own birth). Blond, blue-eyed, and orphaned at an early age, he lived with an elderly aunt and spent his entire life in the Ribatejo countryside. He had only a rudimentary education, and he practiced no profession. Having contracted tuberculosis, he returned to Lisbon in 1915, where he died at the age of twenty-six, rather like Keats.

Despite his unremarkable background and short life, Caeiro occupies a central position in the heteronymous universe; both Reis and Campos refer to him as their *Mestre* [Master], and Pessoa "himself" speaks reverently about him. Here we might note the distinction that Pessoa made repeatedly between the many authors he admired, such as Dickens, and those few such as Cesário Verde and Antero de Quental whom he considered masters, who *ensina[m]* [teach] (3:181) but who are never appreciated during their lifetime (3:183). Caeiro belongs in the second category. Unlike the other heteronyms, he is killed off; for as a master, it is only after his death that the novelty and significance of his poetry can be truly recognized. Pessoa then creates the "disciples" Reis and Campos (as well as the philosopher António Mora), who are "influenced" by Caeiro and who write critical commentaries on his work.

A single chapter affords insufficient space to review all the materials written about Caeiro by the various heteronyms, including Pessoa "himself." These documents were part of an attempt to define what Pessoa called a "new kind of *Weltanschauung*"; nevertheless, they have tended to overshadow the very poems they seek to explicate, which are compelling in their simplicity and their unusual treatment of nature.[3] I would prefer to concentrate more directly on Caeiro's writing, in particular O *Guardador de Rebanhos,* which contains forty-nine poems. His collected works also include the eight poems of the incomplete O *Pastor Amoroso* (The Amorous Shepherd) and the seventy other miscellaneous poems entitled *Poemas Inconjuntos* (Unconnected Poems).[4]

In one sense, Caeiro is an impossible figure: a twentieth-century poet who seems completely untouched by modernity or "civilization." He lives in the countryside and is a bucolic writer whose verses express his absolute respect for the natural world, unburdened by extreme emotion, excessive

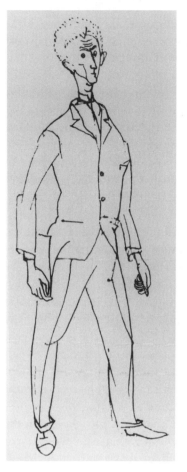

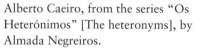

Alberto Caeiro, from the series "Os Heterónimos" [The heteronyms], by Almada Negreiros.

thought, metaphysics, or religion. His straightforwardness is emphasized in the following passage by the translator-heteronym "Thomas Crosse," who introduced Caeiro to an English-speaking audience:

> He sees things with the eyes only, not with the mind. He does not let any thoughts arise when he looks at a flower. Far from seeing sermons in stones, he never even let himself conceive a stone as beginning a sermon. The only sermon a stone contains for him is that it exists. The only thing a stone tells him is that it has nothing at all to tell him. A state of mind may be conceived resembling this. *But it cannot be conceived in a poet . . .* The stupendous fact about Caeiro is that out of this sentiment, or rather, absence of sentiment, he makes poetry. (222–23)

What Caeiro represents is the fairly widespread desire among high-modernist theorists of the period to divest poetry of sentimentality or "rhetoric." We might borrow the words of Ezra Pound in 1912 and say that Caeiro embodies the poet who specializes in the "direct treatment of the thing itself." For the most part, he dispenses with psychology, philosophy, politics, and religion, concentrating on empirical observation. He is a nature poet, but the nature that he observes is little more than the common paraphernalia of literary pastoralism. Because of this artistic minimalism, he becomes a "pure" poet, representing the most fundamental qualities of literariness; as Eliot would say, he treats "poetry as poetry and not another thing."

Caeiro is in some ways like the reaper figure in Pessoa's "Ela canta, pobre ceifeira," which was examined in the previous chapter. Both the reaper and Caeiro are born out of the romantic desire to commune directly with Nature, free of mediating self-consciousness. In "Ela canta, pobre ceifeira," the reaper sings as she works, apparently oblivious of her own happy state; Caeiro is no cheerful peasant, but he writes poems that are critical of the second-order lyricism we find in "Ela canta," where the speaker is always "thinking what he feels." Of course, in the last analysis, Caeiro's "absence of sentiment" and un-self-consciousness are illusory; all of his work is based on the idealized and philosophically dubious notion of a *ding an sich*, or a natural world that the poet can somehow record truthfully by means of an organic fit between signifier and signified.

As we have seen in the previous chapter, Pessoa was intrigued with the relationship between art and emotion, and he formulated a typology of sentiment to rank the different subjective feelings that an artist might express. His ideas on this subject seem to have derived from John Ruskin's famous essay "Of the Pathetic Fallacy" (1865), which evaluated poets according to their ability to "perceive" nature objectively. At one point Ruskin alludes to Wordsworth's poem "Peter Bell: A Tale" in order to make the following distinction:

> So, then, we have the three ranks: the man who perceives rightly, because he does not feel, and to whom the primrose is very accurately the primrose, because he does not love it. Then, secondly, the man who perceives wrongly, because he feels, and to whom the primrose is anything else than a primrose: a star, or a sun, or a fairy's shield, or a forsaken maiden. And then, lastly, there is the man who perceives rightly in spite of his feelings, and to whom the primrose is for ever nothing else than itself—a little flower apprehended in the very plain

and leafy fact of it, whatever and how many soever the associations and passions may be that crowd around it. And, in general, these three classes may be rated in comparative order, as the men who are not poets at all, and the poets of the second order, and the poets of the first.[5]

In an attempt to define Caeiro's ideas about sentiment, Pessoa, under the guise of Álvaro de Campos, records the following exchange between himself and Caeiro about the same Wordsworth poem:

Referindo-me, uma vez, ao conceito directo das coisas, que caracteriza a sensibilidade de Caeiro, citei-lhe, com perversidade amiga, que Wordsworth designa um insensível pela expressão:

A primrose by the river's brim
A yellow primrose was to him,
And it was nothing more.

. . . O meu mestre Caeiro riu. "Esse simples via bem: uma flor amarela não é realmente senão uma flor amarela."

Mas, de repente, pensou.

"Há uma diferença," acrescentou. "Depende se se considera a flor amarela como uma das várias flores amarelas, ou como aquela flor amarela só."

E depois disse:

"O que esse seu poeta inglês queria dizer era que para o tal homem essa flor amarela era uma experiência vulgar, ou uma coisa conhecida. Ora isso é que não está bem. Toda a coisa que vemos, devemos vê-la sempre pela primeira vez, porque realmente é a primeira vez que a vemos. E então cada flor amarela é uma nova flor amarela, ainda que seja o que se chama a mesma de ontem. A gente não é já o mesmo nem a flor a mesma. O próprio amarelo não pode ser já o mesmo. É pena a gente não ter exactamente os olhos para saber isso, porque então eramos todos felizes." (157–58)

[Referring once to the direct perception of things that characterizes the sensibility of Caeiro, I quoted for him with a friendly perversity Wordsworth's poetic description of an insensible being:

A primrose by the river's brim
A primrose was to him,

And it was nothing more.

My master Caeiro laughed. "That simple soul saw well: a yellow flower is really nothing but a yellow flower."

But, suddenly, he thought.

"There's a difference," he added. "It depends on whether one considers a yellow flower as one of various yellow flowers or like only that yellow flower."

And then he said:

"What that English poet wanted to show was that the yellow flower had become a common experience or a known thing to the man. Now that isn't good. Everything we see, we must always see for the first time, because that is when we truly see it. And therefore each yellow flower is a new yellow flower, even though it be the same one named yesterday. People are no longer the same nor is the flower the same. Even the yellow can no longer be the same. It's a pity that people don't have exactly the eyes to know this, because then we would all be happy."]

Caeiro is an instance of Ruskin's poet of the first order, who has "entire command of himself, and can look around calmly, at all moments, for the image of the word that best tells what he sees." Caeiro also embodies what Ruskin describes as the "highest power in a writer," which is "to check all such habits of thought, and to keep his eyes fixed firmly on the *pure fact,* out of which if any feeling comes to him or his reader, he knows it must be a true one." In this sense he is the antithesis of the poets of the second order, who are "subdued by the feelings under which they write . . . and therefore admit certain expressions and modes of thought which are in some sort diseased or false"; as well as the "inspired poets" or urban-weary romantics, who looked to nature as a way of representing directly the pain, sorrow, and often turbulent, irrational states of mind brought on by day-to-day living.[6]

As a result, Caeiro's poetry often has a bare, imagist, or haiku-like quality. He feels none of the angst or ennui of much romantic verse, nor does he represent nature as an escape or as a mirror of the poet's state of mind. Nature (meaning simply the objective world) is an unknown entity to be sung, and the "self" is indistinguishable from landscape:

Não sei o que é a Natureza: canto-a.
Vivo no cimo d'um outeiro

Numa casa caiada e sozinha,
E essa é a minha definição. (80)

[I know not what Nature is: I sing it.
I live on the top of a knoll
In a lone whitewashed house,
And this is my definition.]

The quiet, matter-of-fact tone of Caeiro's verse has an extraordinarily lyrical appeal. At times, however, his antisentimental attitude becomes slightly wry if not humorous, and his style is more calculated than it seems at first glance. His use of repetition and his playfulness with words (like *ver* [to see] and *ouvir* [to hear]) are reminiscent of the "conceit" in baroque verse, reduced to a simpler form. The initial stanzas of poem "XXIV" are a good example of this technique:

O que nós vemos das coisas são as coisas.
Porque veríamos nós uma coisa se houvesse outra?
Porque é que ver e ouvir seriam iludirmo-nos
Se ver e ouvir são ver e ouvir?

O essencial é saber ver,
Saber ver sem estar a pensar,
Saber ver quando se vê,
E nem pensar quando se vê
Nem ver quando se pensa. (74)

[What we see in things are things.
Why would we see one thing if there were another?
Why would seeing and hearing be fooling ourselves
If to see and hear is to see and hear?

The essential thing is to know how to see,
To know how to see without thinking,
To know how to see when one sees,
And neither to think when one sees
Nor see when one thinks.]

As the stanzas quoted above clearly demonstrate, Caeiro is far from the humble shepherd-poet that Pessoa's biographical account and the title of his book, O *Guardador de Rebanhos*, might imply. In fact, the poems in O

Guardador are rigorously constructed around a philosophical argument in which objective and subjective experience, or sensory perception and thought, are constantly opposed. Although he lives outside the city, Caeiro knows about civilization. He has read the poets and is aware of metaphysics, Christianity, and modernity, but he wants to expel these things from poetry. Poem "XXVIII" is a good example of his basic theme:

Li hoje quase duas páginas
Do livro d'um poeta místico
E ri como quem tem chorado muito.

Os poetas místicos são filósofos doentes,
E os filósofos são homens doidos.

Porque os poetas místicos dizem que as flores sentem
E dizem que as pedras têm alma
E que os rios têm êxtases ao luar.

Mas as flores, se sentissem, não eram flores,
Eram gente;
E se as pedras tivessem alma, eram coisas vivas, não eram pedras;
E se os rios tivessem êxtases ao luar,
Os rios seriam homens doentes.

É preciso não saber o que são flores e pedras e rios
Para falar dos sentimentos deles.

Falar da alma das pedras, das flores, dos rios,
É falar de si próprio e dos seus falsos pensamentos.
Graças a Deus que as pedras são só pedras,
E que os rios não são senão rios,
E que as flores são apenas flores.

Por mim, escrevo a prosa dos meus versos
E fico contente,
Porque sei que compreendo a Natureza por fora;
E não a compreendo por dentro
Porque a Natureza não tem dentro;
Senão não era a Natureza. (78)

[Today I read almost two pages
Of a book by a mystic poet
And I laughed like someone who had been crying a lot.

Mystic poets are sick philosophers,
And philosophers are madmen.

Because mystic poets say that flowers feel
And they say that rocks have souls
And that rivers are ecstatic by moonlight.

But flowers, if they felt, wouldn't be flowers,
They'd be people.
And if rocks had souls, they'd be living things, not rocks;
And if the rivers were ecstatic by moonlight,
They would be sick men.

You have to be ignorant of what flowers, rocks and rivers are
In order to speak of their feelings.

To speak of the soul of rocks, flowers, rivers
Is to speak of one's self and of one's false thoughts.
Thank God that rocks are only rocks,
And that the rivers are but rivers,
And that flowers are only flowers.

As for me, I write the prose of my verses
And I am content,
Because I know I understand Nature from the outside,
And do not understand it from within
Because Nature has no within;
Otherwise it wouldn't be Nature.]

Notice that the argument of this poem is somewhat disingenuous. By denying lyricism, Caeiro allows it to come into his verses indirectly; the rocks,
rivers, and trees still have a "soul," if only a negative one, and the poem
depends not on simple description but on assertion.

Exactly the same emotional trick underlies the longer and in some ways
even more remarkable poem "VIII," in which Caeiro describes a dream of
Jesus Christ coming down to earth in the person of an ordinary village
child. The poem's rhetorical force derives from the way it repeatedly juxta-
poses the beautiful innocence of the boy, who wipes his runny nose and
throws stones at donkeys, with the pompous and aging characters of Christian myth. In heaven, the poem asserts, one must be serious, and God is a
"velho estúpido e doente, / Sempre a escarrar no chão / E a dizer inde-
cências" [a stupid, sick old man, / Always spitting on the ground / And

uttering obscenities] (55). The deity who appears to Caeiro is therefore the "Criança Eterna" [Eternal Child] (56), not the man on the cross with the crown of thorns and with nails hammered into his feet ("Com uma coroa toda à roda de espinhos / E os pés espetados por um prego com cabeça" [53]). Notice that this partial denunciation of Christianity allows Caeiro to invest the village landscape with a kind of Christian aura. The poem is paradoxical, because at the very moment that it decries metaphysics and insists on the sheer phenomenological beauty of the world, it generates what Freud would call the "oceanic" feeling of religious wonder.

Just as Caeiro eschews sentiment and metaphysics in poetry, so he also tries to find words that will render the object "directly," and he employs different strategies to keep language at the level of pure denotation: he refrains from metaphor; he avoids modifiers as much as possible; he restricts himself to a limited vocabulary that is repeated in poem after poem; and he negates every lyrical emotion he describes. The sparseness of his verses has nothing to do with a lack of erudition; on the contrary, Caeiro's minimalism is the sign of his rarefied aesthetic desire to strip language down to some core of meaning. But this project is impossible. Despite his efforts, he recognizes that "man's" words will always be, on some level, different from the things they represent:

Só a Natureza é divina, e ela não é divina . . .

Se às vezes falo dela como de um ente
É que para falar dela preciso usar da linguagem dos homens
Que dá personalidade às coisas,
E impõe nome às coisas.

Mas as coisas não têm nome nem personalidade:
Existem, e o céu é grande e a terra larga,
E o nosso coração do tamanho de um punho fechado . . .

Bendito seja eu por tudo quanto não sei.
É isso tudo que verdadeiramente sou.
Gozo tudo isso como quem está aqui ao sol. (77)

[Only Nature is divine, and she is not divine . . .

If at times I speak of her like a thing
It's because in order to speak of her I need to use the language of
      men
That gives personality to things,
And imposes names on things.

But things have neither name nor personality:
They exist, and the sky is large and the earth wide,
And our hearts the size of a closed fist . . .

Blessed be I for all that I do not know.
It is all this that I truly am.
I delight in all this like one who is here in the sun.]

Caeiro's protestations to the contrary, his poems *are* thoughtful meditations, and they are artfully constructed. They lack end rhyme or uniform
meter, but they have a cadence and internal rhyme derived from the repetition of individual words and often whole phrases. In spite of their free-verse
form, they are reminiscent of medieval lyrics, especially when they employ
more-uniform patterns of repetition and internal rhyme. An excellent example of the parallelistic strategy found in many early *cantigas* [songs,
ballads] is poem "XVIII":

Quem me dera que eu fosse o pó da estrada
E que os pés dos pobre me estivessem pisando . . .

Quem me dera que eu fosse os rios que correm
E que as lavadeiras estivessem à minha beira . . .

Quem me dera que eu fosse os choupos à margem do rio
E tivesse só o céu por cima e a água por baixo . . .

Que me dera que eu fosse o burro do moleiro
E que ele me batesse e me estimasse . . .

Antes isso que ser o que atravessa a vida
Olhando para trás de si e tendo pena . . . (67)

[Would that I were the dust on the road
And that the feet of the poor were to tread upon me . . .

Would that I were the rivers that flow
And that washerwomen were at my edge . . .

Would that I were the poplars on the riverbank
And that I had but the sky above and the water below . . .

Would that I were the miller's mule
And that he would beat me yet esteem me . . .

Rather this than to be the one who goes through life
Looking back and feeling regret . . .]

Poem "X" in *O Guardador* resembles a "tenção de briga" [duel of words], which was a variation on the *cantigas* of a satirical nature ("de escárnio e de maldizer") performed by troubadours.[7] It has none of the ribaldry associated with this form, but it presents a dialogue between an anonymous, "inspired" individual and Caeiro, who "checks all such habits of thought":

"Olá, guardador de rebanhos,
Aí à beira da estrada,
Que te diz o vento que passa?"

"Que é vento, e que passa,
E que já passou antes,
E que passará depois.
E a ti o que te diz?"

"Muita coisa mais do que isso.
Fala-me de muitas outras coisas.
De memórias e de saudades
E de coisas que nunca foram."

"Nunca ouviste passar o vento.
O vento só fala do vento.
O que lhe ouviste foi mentira,
E a mentira está em ti." (59)

["Hello, keeper of sheep,
There at the side of the road,
What does the passing wind say to you?"

"That it's wind, and that it passes,
And that it already passed before,
And that it will pass again.
And to you what does it say?"

"Many more things than that.
It speaks to me of many other things.
Of memories and longings
And things that never were."

"You never heard the wind pass by.
The wind only speaks of the wind.
What you heard was a lie,
And the lie is in you."]

Here as elsewhere, Caeiro makes use of free verse, and, partly for that reason, scholars have written at length about the similarities between him and Whitman. There can be no doubt that Whitman was a major influence on Pessoa—just as he was for many other modernists, including Pound. But it should be noted that Whitman drew inspiration from the Psalms and Song of Songs, whereas Pessoa/Caeiro's sources seem to derive from medieval songs. Whitman is a powerful lyric poet who demonstrates a deep tenderness and lofty spirituality while Caeiro, like Pessoa's theoretical "general," keeps his sentiments at bay. Unlike Whitman, Caeiro is not concerned with progress, democracy, or the utopian community of nature, humanity, and God. He has no special interest in his fellow beings: "Que me importam a mim os homens / E o que sofrem ou supõem que sofrem?" [What does mankind matter to me? / And what they suffer or suppose that they suffer] (82); and, at best, he is skeptical of God: "Não acredito no Deus porque nunca o vi" [I don't believe in God because I have never seen him] (49). He even denies the existence of nature as an idealized concept: "Vi que não há Natureza, / Que Natureza não existe . . . [I saw that there is no Nature / That Nature doesn't exist] (98). The humanist Whitman gathers up everything and everyone in reach, embracing them as part of his self and his world. By contrast, Caeiro writes: "Ser poeta não é uma ambição minha. / É a minha maneira de estar sozinho" [To be a poet is not my ambition. / It's my way of being alone] (42).[8]

As a literary construction, Caeiro seems more like the Portuguese poet Cesário Verde, who recorded with a lyrical exactitude the sights and sounds of nineteenth-century Lisbon. In poems like Verde's "Cristalizações" [Crystallizations], for example, one can see an incipient Caeiro, particularly in the emphasis on "clarity" and the important role of the senses:

Eu tudo encontro alegremente exacto.
Lavo, refresco, limpo os sentidos.
E tangem-me, excitados, sacudidos,
O tacto, a vista, o ouvido, o gosto, o olfacto![9]

[I find everything happily exact.
I wash, refresh, cleanse my senses.
And my touch, sight, hearing,
and taste, excited and shaken, sound within me!]

Cesário Verde was a protomodernist who was fascinated by city types, and who employed a subject matter not usually associated with poetry. He wrote about *engomadeiras* (women who starch and iron clothes), calkers, fishwives, dentists, and shop windows in such a strikingly new way that Portuguese poetry was never quite the same after him. Pessoa's heteronym Álvaro de Campos, who writes about hoists, cranes, and tobacco shops, is certainly in Verde's debt—but so is Caeiro in a more abstract way. Throughout, Caeiro questions what constitutes the language of poetry; in his rejection of "inspired" verse, he is constantly attempting to write in a "cleansed" fashion—however impossible that goal may be. One often feels that he wants to achieve pure, unreflective consciousness, shedding even the name and personality of Alberto Caeiro:

> Procuro despir-me do que aprendi,
> Procuro esquecer-me do modo de lembrar que me ensinaram,
> E raspar a tinta com que me pintaram os sentidos,
> Desencaixotar as minhas emoções verdadeiras,
> Desembrulhar-me e ser eu, não Alberto Caeiro,
> Mas um animal humano que a Natureza produziu. (97)

> [I seek to divest myself of what I learned,
> I seek to forget the way of remembering that they taught me,
> And to scrape away the paint with which they colored my senses,
> To unbox my true emotions,
> To unwrap myself and be me, not Alberto Caeiro,
> But a human animal that Nature produced.]

Of all the heteronyms, Caeiro is perhaps Pessoa's most radical creation. Like Shakespeare's Hamlet, he is a fiction, but a fiction so improbable that it seems like a myth. Pessoa called him the "master"; he is certainly the most self-assured of the various authors, but that does not necessarily mean that he was the best or the greatest. He was simply the "pure" poet—the simple, direct versifier who set a minimal standard for good writing. The other heteronyms would build on his achievement, adding complex verse forms and giving philosophical and psychological range to their art. Caeiro came first in the order of things, much as the imagist and free-verse experiments of early British modernism preceded more difficult writings of the 1920s. Caeiro was therefore Pessoa's way of dramatizing the basic requirements of good literature, before it could aspire to any broad commentary on the world.

The Poetry of Ricardo Reis

Pessoa said that once Caeiro had appeared to him in March of 1914, he instinctively and subconsciously created a few "disciples"—among them, the modern neoclassicist known as Ricardo Reis. In Pessoa's letter to Casais Monteiro in 1935, he claims that "[a]rranquei do seu falso paganismo o Ricardo Reis latente, descobri-lhe o nome, e ajustei-o a si mesmo, porque nessa altura já o *via*" [I pulled the latent Ricardo Reis from (Caeiro's) false paganism, came up with his name, and adjusted it to him, for at that point I was already *seeing* him] (2:341). (Pessoa also mentions that he had considered writing a "pagan" verse as early as 1912 and that in that moment, without his knowing it, the style of Ricardo Reis had been invented [2:340–41]). As with Caeiro, Pessoa provided some biographical data on Reis, who was born in Oporto in 1887 (one year prior to Pessoa), was educated by Jesuits, and was a practicing physician. A monarchist, Reis left Portugal in 1919 and moved to Brazil. Pessoa described him as dark and a little shorter and stronger than Caeiro but with a drier manner (2:343).

According to a fragmentary statement written in 1914, Pessoa actually invented Ricardo Reis some months prior to the time announced in the letter to Casais Monteiro. The importance of this fragment has less to do with the dates of Reis's "birth," however, than with Pessoa's comment about a discussion that he heard on "the excesses of modern art," which seems to have given him the idea for the Reis heteronym:

O Dr. Ricardo Reis nasceu dentro da minha alma no dia 29 de Janeiro de 1914, pelas 11 horas da noite. Eu estivera ouvindo no dia anterior uma discussão extensa sobre os excessos, especialmente de realização, da arte moderna. Segundo o meu processo de sentir as coisas sem as sentir, fui-me deixando ir na onda dessa reacção momentânea. Quando reparei em que estava pensando, vi que tinha erguido uma teoria neo-clássica, e que a ia desenvolvendo. Achei-a bela e calculei interessante se a desenvolvesse segundo princípios que não adopto nem aceito. Ocorreu-me a ideia de a tornar um neoclassicismo "científico" . . . reagir contra duas correntes—tanto contra o romantismo moderno, como contra o neoclassicismo à Maurras. (2:1067–68)

[Dr. Ricardo Reis was born in my soul on the 29th day of January in 1914, around 11 o'clock at night. The day before, I had been listening to an extensive discussion on the excesses, especially in the formation, of modern art. In keeping with my process of feeling things without being aware of feeling them, I allowed myself to ride the wave of this momentary reaction. When I noticed what I was thinking about, I saw that I had constructed a neoclassic theory and was continuing to develop it. I found it beautiful and thought it interesting if I developed it according to principles that I myself neither adopt nor accept. The idea occurred to me to make it a "scientific" neoclassicism . . . reacting against two currents—as much against modern romanticism as against neoclassicism in the manner of Maurras.]

As I have already observed in chapter 3, much of Pessoa's work can be understood in terms of a dialectical tension between the "classic" and "ro-

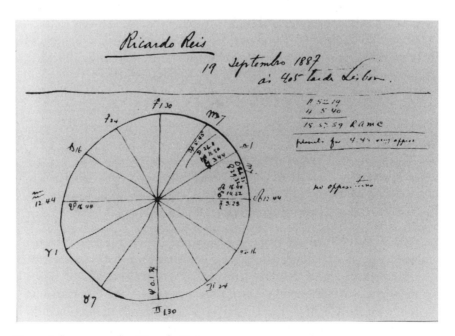

Pessoa's horoscope for Ricardo Reis.

mantic" strains of modernism. Here he makes that tension explicit; at the same time, he explains that the neoclasssic heteronym Ricardo Reis functions as a corrective to the influential French critic and polemicist Charles Maurras (1868–1952), who was associated with what came to be known as "revolutionary classicism." The protofascist Maurras was an intellectual forerunner of the British theorist T. E. Hulme and was in some respects the founder of an archconservative, antirationalist tendency we can find in high modernism throughout Europe.[1] Maurras was, however, more of a political figure than a literary type, and his anti-Semitism was not shared by Pessoa. (Similarly, Pessoa had remained distant from the "romantic" firebrand Marinetti.) As a result, Pessoa responds by creating a conservative modernist who embodies certain virtues from the age of rationalism and Enlightenment.

On a more general level, Pessoa's desire to create a heteronym like Reis is in keeping with his respect for literary tradition and his long-standing fascination with classical antiquity. As we know from scholars Alexandrino Severino and H. D. Jennings as well as from biographer João Gaspar Simões, Pessoa was trained in the classics, and his interest in Ancient Greece and Rome can be seen everywhere in his prose fragments and essays—not to mention in the verse that he wrote under the name of Pessoa "himself." After the demise of *Orpheu,* Pessoa founded another literary review with a classical title, *Athena,* in which, in 1924, he first published several of the more than one hundred odes he would ultimately pen under the name of Ricardo Reis.

Anyone familiar with eighteenth-century Portuguese verse can see the affinities between Reis and those neoclassic writers who, reacting against the excesses of the Baroque and inspired by the Enlightenment, wrote poems in imitation of the ancients. The official date of *arcadismo,* or Portuguese neoclassicism, is 1756, when a group of writers in Lisbon founded an "Arcádia Lusitana" in imitation of the Roman Arcadia of 1690. For these poets, Arcadia, the mountainous area in Greece, epitomized rustic simplicity. The sixteenth-century Italian Sannazzaro's novel *Arcadia,* about pastoral life and poetry, became a model for what the new movement hoped to achieve. A principal motif of *arcadismo* was the *locus amoenus* of the countryside; thus, poets like Padre Francisco Manuel do Nascimento, better known as "Filinto Elísio," adopted Latinate pseudonyms, calling themselves "shepherds" and composing verses to maidens who were addressed as shepherdess-muses. Alberto Caeiro was in some respects modeled on this eighteenth-century notion of the ancient poet, although Caeiro's verse is not severely "classic" or imitative in form or content.

Clarity and "noble" simplicity, or *inutilia truncat,* were among the primary goals of eighteenth-century literature. Poetry was the most respected genre of the period, and the most fashionable verse forms were the eclogue, the sonnet, and the ode. An epicurist and stoic, the typical *arcadista* strove to achieve the Horatian ideal of the *aurea mediocritas,* focusing on the simplest pleasures, the peacefulness of nature, and the transitoriness of life. Two of the most celebrated authors of this period were the poets Tomás António Gonzaga and Manuel Maria Barbosa du Bocage, who brought to their work a characteristic precision and pure style together with an intimate, rather subjective quality.[2] Formally and thematically, Ricardo Reis is very much within this neoclassic mold: he writes Horatian odes about the necessity of maintaining calm in the face of mortality, about the vulnerability of humans in contrast to the gods, and about the repudiation of emotional extremes in favor of a measured tranquillity.[3] Several of his poems are addressed to women, who, in their pastoral guise as "Nise," "Cloe," or "Neera," function as both muse and ear for stoic meditations on the small pleasures to be enjoyed in a world filled with adversities. He writes from the *locus amoenus* of the countryside, and he draws his metaphors from nature and classical mythology. Unlike many of his predecessors, however, his compositions tend to be sad if not remorseful, and his personal calm seems induced rather than natural. As his "brother," the heteronym "Frederico Reis" once declared: "A obra de Ricardo Reis, profundamente triste, é um esforço lúcido e disciplinado para obter uma calma qualquer" [Profoundly sad, the work of Ricardo Reis is a lucid and disciplined effort, striving to achieve whatever calm it can] (2:1068).

It is in his ideal of calm lucidity that Reis most resembles Caeiro. In one ode, he proclaims that the gods can take everything away from him—love, glory, riches—if only they will leave him "[a] consciência lúcida e solene / Das coisas e dos seres" [the lucid and solemn consciousness / Of things and beings] (1:825). Also, like Caeiro, he often feels a special oneness with nature: " . . . Aquele arbusto / Fenece, e vai com ele / Parte da minha vida. / Em tudo quanto olhei fiquei em parte" [. . . That bush / Withers, and with it / Part of my life. / In all that I saw a part of me remained] (1:847). Yet there are significant differences between the two poets. Caeiro's attitude toward life seems healthy, almost robust, because of his innate "innocence" and lack of civilized self-consciousness. He is virtually immune to human suffering or to injustices because he identifies exclusively with the natural world, where living and dying are immutable and acceptable facts. Free of doubts or anxieties, he is *naturally* reconciled to his environment and is philosophically unconcerned about whether he feels happy or sad. (The only things that seem to disturb Caeiro at all are other poets—namely the ones who "see sermons in stones.") He is a "pagan" or non-Christian, but at the same time, he writes poems in which nature sometimes manifests a godlike quality. His language is somewhat austere and dignified, but it is also simple and proselike, as if he were responding freely to sensations. Reis, on the other hand, brings considerable psychological and literary baggage with him to the provinces. He is riddled with anxieties, and because he is a "medical doctor" who is constantly faced with suffering and death, his odes have a special poignancy. Frequently, he conveys a sense of emotion held under control. He also writes poems in which the traditional bittersweet urgency of a *carpe diem* is transformed into a stiff-upper-lip reserve:

Ao longe os montes têm neve ao sol,
Mas é suave já o frio calmo
    Que alisa e agudece
    Os dardos do sol alto.

Hoje, Neera, não nos escondamos,
Nada nos falta, porque nada somos.
    Não esperamos nada
    E temos frio ao sol.

Mas tal como é, gozemos o momento,
Solenes na alegria levemente,
    E aguardando a morte
    Como quem a conhece. (1:812)

[In the distance the mountains are snow-covered in the sunlight
But the calm cold is already soft
    That smoothes and sharpens
    The shafts of the midday sun.

Today, Neera, let us not hide ourselves,
We lack nothing because we are nothing.
    We hope for nothing
    And we are cold in the sunlight.

But such as it is, let us enjoy the moment,
Lightly solemn in our joy,
    And awaiting death
    Like one who knows it.]

In such poems Reis departs significantly from his eighteenth-century models, who often wrote about the fleeting nature of life. Consider the following verses, by the neoclassic poet Gonzaga, whose "Dirceu" speaks to his love, "Marília":

> Ah! enquanto os destinos impiedosos
> não voltam contra nós a face irada,
> façamos, sim, façamos, doce amada,
> os nossos breves dias mais ditosos.
> Um coração que, frouxo,
> a grata posse de seu bem difere,
> a si, Marília, a si próprio rouba,
> e a si próprio fere.
>
> Ornemos nossas testas com as flores,
> e façamos de feno um brando leito;
> prendamo-nos, Marília, em laço estreito,
> gozemos do prazer de sãos amores.
> Sobre as nossas cabeças,
> sem que o possam deter, o tempo corre;
> e para nós o tempo que se passa
> também, Marília, morre.[4]

> [Ah! while the ruthless fates
> turn not toward us their angry faces,
> let us, my love, yes, let us make
> our fleeting days all the more joyful.
> A weak-willed heart
> that postpones the grateful possession of its welfare
> robs itself, its very self, Marília,
> and wounds itself.
>
> Let us adorn our foreheads with flowers,
> and let us make of hay a yielding bed;
> let us cling together, Marília, in a tight embrace,
> let us enjoy the pleasure of healthy love.
> Above our heads,
> time passes without our ability to deter it;
> and for us the time that passes,
> Marília, it too shall perish.]

In poem after poem by Gonzaga, Dirceu pours out his heart to Marília and longs to make love. In similar fashion, the eighteenth-century poet Bocage, who went by the pseudonym Elmano Sadino, conveys a good deal of sensuality and desire. Here, for example, are the final stanzas of his epistle "Elmano a Urselina" [From Elmano to Urselina]:

> Vive sempre ditosa entre meus braços,
> Vive em serena paz, e adeus, querida,
> Que para a morte já dirijo os passos.
> Ela chama por mim, vou dar-lhe a vida:
> Feliz eu, no fim míscro a que aspiro,
> Se coa boca amorosa à tua unida
> Desentranhasse meu final suspiro![5]

> [Live always gladly in my embrace,
> Live in serene peace, and farewell, beloved,
> For I'm already guiding my steps toward death.
> She calls for me, I'll give her my life:
> Happy will I be, in the miserable end to which I aspire,
> If with my loving mouth with yours joined
> I were to draw from the depths my final breath!]

In one of his especially passionate sonnets, Bocage questions why "Reason" is unable to put out his flame:

> Razão, de que me serve o teu socorro?
> Mandas-me não amar, eu ardo, eu amo;
> Dizes-me que sossegue, eu peno, eu morro.[6]

> [Reason, what good does your help do me?
> You order me not to love, yet I'm on fire, I love;
> You tell me to be calm, yet I'm in pain, I'm dying.]

Perhaps what Pessoa was suggesting when he referred to Reis as a "scientific" neoclassicist was that there is a nearly total absence of passion and physical love in Reis's verse. If we look to Reis's role-model, Caeiro, we find a similar quality—indeed Caeiro appears not to know that women exist. The sole exception to this rule are the six poems of O Pastor Amoroso, in which the poet refers obliquely to an indefinite "she." Interestingly, in his preface to Caeiro's work, Reis is highly critical of this small body of verse, claiming it was the product of "um breve episódio, improfícuo e absurdo . . . um esqueci-mento" [a brief, futile, and absurd episode . . . a heedlessness].[7] For Reis, all forms of intense emotion—physical love in particular—are undesirable. In one ode, he proclaims that love places "limits" on the "cold liberty" that he most desires; and in another, he is quite explicit about the need to reject any sort of amorous entanglements: "Não quero, Cloe, teu amor, que oprime / Porque me exige o amor. Quero ser livre" [I do not want, Cloe, your love which oppresses / Because it demands love of me. I want to be free] (1:851).

Reis is at best a reluctant suitor who prefers that a woman sit quietly by his side, avoiding intimate contact:

Vem sentar-te comigo, Lídia, à beira do rio.
Sossegadamente fitemos o seu curso e aprendamos
Que a vida passa, e não estamos de mãos enlaçadas.
    (Enlacemos as mãos.)
           . . .
Desenlacemos as mãos, porque não vale a pena cansarmo-nos.
Quer gozemos, quer não gozemos, passamos como o rio.
Mais vale saber passar silenciosamente
    E sem desassossegos grandes.

Sem amores, nem ódios, nem paixões que levantam a voz,
Nem invejas que dão movimento demais aos olhos,
Nem cuidados, porque se os tivesse o rio sempre correria,
    E sempre iria ter ao mar.

Amemo-nos tranquilamente, pensando que podíamos,
Se quiséssemos, trocar beijos e abraços e carícias,
Mas que mais vale estarmos sentados ao pé um do outro
    Ouvindo correr o rio e vendo-o . . . (1:811–12)

[Come sit down with me, Lídia, on the bank of the river.
Let us quietly watch its course and learn
That life passes by, and we are not holding hands.
    (Let us hold hands.)
           . . .
Let us release our hands because it is not worth tiring ourselves.
Whether we enjoy or do not enjoy, we pass by like the river.
It is worth more to know how to silently pass by
    Without great disquiet.

Without loves, or hates, or passions that raise the voice,
Or envies that give too much movement to the eyes,
Or concerns, because even if the river had them, it would always flow,
    And would always join with the sea.

Let us love one another tranquilly, thinking that we could,
    If we wished, exchange kisses and embraces and caresses,
But what is worth more is our sitting next to one another,
        Listening to the river flow and watching it . . .]

This particular ode concludes with the poet celebrating the fact that he has
never held the woman's hand or kissed her. Because he has not experienced
physical contact, he says he will not suffer the pain of romantic loss when
he eventually goes to his deathbed. (One of the more touching yet morbid
odes in the collection, "A nada imploram tuas mãos já coisas" [To nothing
do your hands, now things, implore], is, in fact, about a dead woman
whom the poet imagines lying in the grave with the trace of a smile on her
face.)

The distance that Reis repeatedly keeps between himself and his female
muses is similar in many ways to the emotional reserve we find in the poetry
of Pessoa "himself," who writes about conventional female figures such as
the reaper and the consumptive maiden and who deals with sexual love
only in the most abstract fashion. In fact, among "Pessoa's" poems is one
that uses roughly the same dramatic situation as Reis's ode quoted above;
here, however, the poet wants simply to be left alone:

Não venhas sentar-te à minha frente, nem a meu lado;
        Não venhas falar, nem sorrir.
Estou cansado de tudo, estou cansado,
        Quero só dormir.
                . . .
Por isso, se vieres, não sentes a meu lado, nem fales.
        Só quero dormir, uma morte que seja
Uma coisa que me não rale nem com que tu te rales—
        Que ninguém deseja nem não deseja. (1:240)

[Don't come and sit in front of me or beside me;
        Don't come and talk or smile.
I'm tired of everything, I'm tired,
        I want only to sleep.
                . . .
Thus, if you come, don't sit down beside me or talk.
        I want only to sleep, a death that is
A thing which doesn't irritate me or irritate you—
        That no one wants or doesn't want.]

Unlike Pessoa "himself," who is sick of "thinking" and who prefers sleep or death to companionship, Reis seldom turns completely away from the world. Through the more elevated style of his ode, he is able to delicately bypass passion for a peaceful (nonsexual) coexistence; in the process, he deftly circumvents the frustration and despair of Pessoa's "own" verse. There are times, however, when even the stoical Reis succumbs to fatalistic tendencies and the voices of the two poets sound almost as one. For example, here is a short poem by Reis, dated September 1932:

> Nada fica de nada. Nada somos.
> Um pouco ao sol e ao ar nos atrasamos
> Da irrespirável treva que nos pese
> Da humilde terra imposta,
> Cadáveres adiados que procriam.
>
> Leis feitas, estátuas vistas, odes findas—
> Tudo tem cova sua. Se nós, carnes
> A que um íntimo sol dá sangue, temos
> Poente, por que não elas?
> Somos contos contando contos, nada. (1:856)

> [Nothing leaves nothing. We are nothing.
> In the sun and air we delay ourselves a bit
> From the unbreathable darkness that will weigh us down
> Imposed by the humble ground,
> Postponed cadavers that procreate.
>
> Laws made, statues seen, odes finished—
> Everything has its own grave. If we, flesh
> To which an intimate sun gives blood, if we have
> A sunset, why don't they?
> We are stories telling stories, nothing.]

Just months after writing this ode, Pessoa "himself" penned his famous poem about the mad Dom Sebastião in *Mensagem*. Here we find the same image of the "living corpse":

> Minha loucura, outros que me a tomem
> Com o que nela ia.
> Sem a loucura que é o homem
> Mais que a besta sadia
> Cadáver adiado que procria? (1:1152)

[My madness, let others take it from me
With what it held inside.
Without madness what is man
Except a healthy beast
A postponed corpse that procreates?]

There are even greater similarities between Reis's ode and another poem written by "Pessoa" just one month after the "Dom Sebastião" composition:

Indiferente assisto
Ao cadaverizar
Do que sou.
Em que alma ou corpo existo?
Vou dormir ou despertar?
Onde estou se não estou?

Nada. É na treva onde fala
O relógio fatal,
Uma grande, anónima sala,
Uma grande treva onde se cala,
Um grande bem que sabe a mal,
Uma vida que se desiguala,
Uma morte que não sabe a que é igual. (1:351)

[Indifferent, I attend
The cadaverizing
Of what I am.
In which soul or body do I exist?
Will I asleep or awaken?
Where am I if I am not?

Nothing. It is in the darkness where
The fatal clock speaks,
A great, anonymous room,
A great darkness where one falls silent,
A great good that tastes like grief,
A life that renders itself unequal to itself,
A death that does not know that to which it is equal.]

Thus, in certain moods, both Reis and Pessoa "himself" are resigned to their lot as living cadavers awaiting the ultimate darkness *(treva)*, or death.

In the examples that I have just cited, Pessoa "himself" seems more Reis-like than usual about *Nada* or fate ("Indiferente assisto"); whereas Reis, who is generally able to keep calm in the face of inevitable death, appears uncharacteristically pessimistic ("Nada somos"). What, then, distinguishes these two lyric poets from each other? In this particular instance, I would argue that the distinctions are mostly stylistic. Reis writes in blank verse, and his references to "statues" and "odes" place his work in the classical tradition. Because he is a neoclassicist, his syntax is more complex than "Pessoa's" and his images tend to be more recondite. In contrast, "Pessoa" uses end rhymes and repetitions, harking back to a tradition of folk literature. His language is simpler than Reis's, although he does introduce a wonderful neologism, *cadaverizar.*

In important ways, the two poets represent quite similar personalities: they are equally traditional, equally reserved in their emotions, and equally given to dark moods. Just as "Pessoa" is deeply indebted to nineteenth-century Portuguese romanticism, Reis is indebted to eighteenth-century Portuguese neoclassicism. But Reis is also presented as a disciple of Caeiro—an improbable figure who writes poems free of personal emotions or any kind of self-consciousness. What distinguishes Reis from the original neoclassics is his wish to feel *no* emotion. He does not imitate the more passionate, even bawdy, verses of Horace; nor does he pen elevated love poems in the fashion of most eighteenth-century poets. Much like Caeiro, whose serene disposition and objectivity he admires, Reis seems to reject physical love altogether. In doing so, he also avoids the sort of intense subjectivity and preoccupation with sex that we find everywhere in "romantic" modernism. At the same time, he has no overtly religious or political agenda such as we find in conservative or "classic" modernism. It is as if Pessoa, through Reis, were attempting to avoid all the extremes of the twentieth century and to find yet another way to write poems without giving over to emotion. The results are a rather narrowly academic kind of verse and a growing need to express a romantic personality in the form of his most flamboyant heteronym, Álvaro de Campos.

6

The Poetry of Álvaro de Campos

Pessoa wrote to Casais Monteiro, "[P]us em Álvaro de Campos toda a emoção que não dou nem a mim nem à vida" [I put into Álvaro de Campos all the emotion that I give neither to myself nor to life] (2:338). And, indeed, unlike any of the other heteronyms, Campos is an engagingly witty and flamboyant personality; he writes about sex and drugs, he smokes incessantly, he experiences hallucinations, and he seems always to be riding a roller coaster of emotion. He is an utterly urbane character (he even wears a monocle) who has traveled to far-off places like the Orient and has no special affinity with the provinces, despite having been "born" there. As he states in his celebrated poem, "Tabacaria" [Tobacco Shop]: "Fui até ao campo com grandes propósitos. / Mas lá encontrei só ervas e árvores" [I went as far as the countryside with great intentions. / But there I found only grass and trees] (1:961).

Campos's importance to the overall project of the heteronyms is suggested by the sheer volume of his writings (which exceeds the combined work of Reis and Caeiro) and by the diversity of materials that bear his name. His collected poems, essays, reviews, and manifestos demonstrate almost the same energy and eclecticism as Pessoa's "own" work. There are, in fact, some intimate and psychologically intriguing aspects of the Pessoa–Campos relationship. According to Ángel Crespo's biography, Pessoa once confounded his friend João Gaspar Simões and the poet José Régio by introducing himself as Campos and carrying on an extended conversation with the two men as if he were his heteronym.[1] Shortly after this meeting, Pessoa wrote a personal letter to Simões, remarking in the last lines that the letter had been turned over to Campos to edit (2:286). His practical jokes and games of mystification with the Campos figure extended even into his "flirtation" with a young secretary, Ophélia de Queiroz. Among the "love letters" that he wrote to Ophélia is one bearing Campos's signature. In another letter, he writes, "Não imaginas a graça que te achei hoje à janela da casa da tua irmã! Ainda bem que estavas alegre e que mostraste prazer em me ver (Álvaro de Campos)" [You can't imagine my delight today when I saw you at the window of your sister's house! Even more so that you were happy and showed pleasure in seeing me (Álvaro de Campos)].[2]

Pessoa recounted the genesis of Campos with the same dramatic flair that characterizes the descriptions of his other chief heteronyms: "E, de repente, e em derivação oposta à de Ricardo Reis, surgiu-me impetuosamente um novo indivíduo. Num jacto, e à máquina de escrever, sem interrupção nem emenda, surgiu a *Ode Triunfal* de Álvaro de Campos—a Ode com esse nome e o homem com o nome que tem" [And suddenly, from a source opposite to that of Ricardo Reis, there brashly appeared to me a new individual. At the typewriter, and in a gush without interruption or correction, appeared the *Triumphal Ode* of Álvaro de Campos—the Ode with that title and the man with the name he now bears] (2:341).

It is almost as if the creation of Reis, who was the most repressed and "classicized" of Pessoa's many alter egos, necessitated the creation of his direct opposite—a romantic and modern character who gave voice to all the forces held in check by the other heteronyms. Hence Pessoa gives Campos a rather elaborate biography, explaining to Casais Monteiro that one of his early poems, "Opiário" [Opiarium] represents Campos's style prior to his coming under the influence of Caeiro. At one point he even draws a comparison between himself and the heteronym:

> Álvaro de Campos nasceu em Tavira, no dia 15 de Outubro de 1890 (às 1,30 da tarde, diz me o Ferreira Gomes; e é verdade, pois, feito o horóscopo para essa hora, está certo). Este, como sabe, é engenheiro naval (por Glasgow), mas agora está aqui em Lisboa em inactividade . . . [É] alto (1,75 m de altura, mais 2 cm do que eu), magro e um pouco tendente a curvar-se. Cara rapada . . . entre branco e moreno, tipo vagamente de judeu português, cabelo, porém, liso e normalmente apartado ao lado, monóculo . . . [T]eve uma educação vulgar de liceu; depois foi mandado para a Escócia estudar engenharia, primeiro mecânica e depois naval. Numas férias fez a viagem ao Oriente de onde resultou o *Opiário*. Ensinou-lhe latim um tio beirão que era padre. (2:342–43)

> [Álvaro de Campos was born in Tavira on the 15th day of October in 1890 (at 1:30 in the afternoon, so Gomes Ferreira tells me; and it's true, for having done the horoscope of that hour, that's right). As you know, he's a naval engineer (via Glasgow), but now he's here, not

Signature of Álvaro de Campos.

working, in Lisbon . . . [He] is tall (1.75 meters in height, 2 cm. taller than I), thin and a little prone to stoop. Clean-shaven . . . he's between dark and light, a vaguely Jewish Portuguese type, however with straight hair which is normally parted at the side, and a monocle. [He] had a common high-school education; then he was sent to Scotland to study first mechanical then naval engineering. During one holiday he went to the Orient, which resulted in his *Opiarium*. He was taught Latin by an uncle from the Beira region, who was a priest.]

Pessoa's special interest in Campos was returned in a less-generous fashion by the heteronym, who is the only one of Pessoa's creations to acknowledge Fernando Pessoa to any degree. In his essays, Campos occasionally commented on Pessoa's work, about which he tended to be less than enthusiastic. In 1915, he penned an amusing "review" in verse entitled "A Fernando Pessoa: Depois de Ler o Seu Drama Estático 'O Marinheiro' em 'Orpheu I'" [To Fernando Pessoa: After reading his static drama "The Sailor" in "Orpheu I"]:

> Depois de doze minutos
> Do seu drama O *Marinheiro,*
> Em que os mais ágeis e astutos
> Se sentem com sono e brutos,
> E de sentido nem cheiro,
> Diz uma das veladoras
> Com langorosa magia

> *De eterno e belo há apenas o sonho.*
> *Por que estamos nós falando ainda?*

Ora isso mesmo é que eu ia
Perguntar a essas senhoras . . . (1:929)

[After twelve minutes
Of his drama *The Sailor,*
Which make the most agile and astute
Feel sleepy and brutish,
And mystified as to the meaning,
One of the women says
With languid magic

Of the eternal and beautiful there is only the dream.
Why are we still speaking?

Now that is exactly what I was going
To ask of these women . . .]

We know from Pessoa's comments that he regarded Campos as a "disciple" of Caeiro but also as the "opposite" of Reis. Pessoa does not elaborate on this opposition, but even a cursory examination of the two poets' respective odes would reveal the obvious difference between them. Reis tends to write short, blank-verse poems about passing time and the small pleasures of life in the countryside. His style is elevated, untouched by the vernacular, and completely derived from the pastoral conventions of the eighteenth century. Campos, on the other hand, writes long, free-verse odes in which factories, steamships, and all sorts of modern commerce merge with images of Portugal's seafaring past. His mood is sometimes lofty, even ecstatic; his style, however, is colloquial, profane, bordering on the stream-of-consciousness.[3] Most of all, the two heteronyms differ from each other in terms of their emotional temperaments. Reis's poetry is nearly always measured, quiet, and stoic; Campos's work ranges in tone from the wildly euphoric to the suicidally depressed.

Campos is a fascinating personality in part because he enables Pessoa to express the vital connection between early modernism and modernity itself. Without Campos, Pessoa would seem a much less cosmopolitan and innovative figure, and the modernist movement in Portugal as a whole would seem less exciting. But Campos is also fascinating because of his formal and psychological complexity. With the exception of Pessoa "himself," he is the only heteronym to actually *evolve* as a poet. Early in his "career," he writes two sonnets that could easily pass for Pessoa's "own" lyrics. By the same token, his early poem on the Orient, "Opiário" (1914), is a series of rhymed quatrains that deal with the same themes of emotional disquiet and tedium that we find everywhere in the work of Pessoa "himself." In fact, there are allusions to Pessoa's own biography in this poem:

E fui criança como toda a gente,
Nasci numa província portuguesa
E tenho conhecido gente inglesa
Que diz que eu sei inglês perfeitamente.

Gostava de ter poemas e novelas
Publicadas por Plon e no *Mercure,*
Mas é impossível que esta vida dure.
Se nesta viagem nem houve procelas! (1:873)

[And I was a child like everyone else,
I was born in a Portuguese province
And I have known English people
Who say that I know English perfectly.

I liked to have poems and novellas
Published by Plon and in the *Mercure,*
But it is impossible for this life to go on.
If on this voyage there weren't even any storms!]

It is in "Opiário," however, that the seeds of the more volatile, sensationist, and quasi-futurist Campos are also to be found. A naval engineer, Campos is interested in machines; unlike the other heteronyms, he speaks ecstatically of *mecanismos* [mechanisms], *engrenagens* [gears], and *volantes* [fly-wheels; also steering wheels]. At the same time, he is a somewhat Rimbaud-like personality who drinks hard liquor, smokes cigarettes and opium, and injects morphine, while mindlessly crossing between Lisbon and the Orient. At times he seems like a latter-day, out-of-work Portuguese navigator. For the most part, he is an armchair traveler whose journeys are *inward* and nearly always induced by cigarettes and other drugs that fuel his imagination.[4] Like Reis, he seeks "calm," but he cannot seem to discipline his emotions. He is also obsessed by death, which he sometimes welcomes as a release from his *desassossego*, or disquiet. Sitting in a deck chair while crossing the Suez Canal, he proclaims: "Ah que bom que era ir daqui de caída / Pra cova por um alçapão de estouro!" [Ah, how great it would be to drop from here / Straight to the grave through the burst of a trap-door!] (1:877).

"Opiário" opens the way for some of Campos's best-known poems of his second, more radical phase. In chapter 2, I briefly commented on the avant-garde nature of two of these poems, "Ode Triunfal" and "Ode Marítima," which Pessoa neatly contrasted with his own, more-traditional compositions in the first two issues of *Orpheu*. During this radical period, Campos completed some of the most extraordinarily effusive writings in modern Portuguese literature. In contrast to almost everything that Pessoa wrote under other names, these are extremely long compositions ("Ode Marítima" runs to at least thirty pages in most volumes), allowing for a considerable amount of wit, bombast, introspection, and irreverence. As critics have often pointed out, they are reminiscent in many ways of Walt Whitman, a poet whom Pessoa greatly admired and whom he discussed at length in several essays and prefaces. Pessoa often refers to Whitman as *mestre,* comparing and contrasting him with Caeiro; and in Álvaro de Campos he creates a heteronym who not only resembles the American but who also writes an homage entitled "Saudação a Walt Whitman" [Greetings to Walt Whitman].

Stylistically and thematically, Campos is clearly indebted to Whitman, who also was imitated by the French *Unanimistes* and by the avant-guerre modernists throughout Europe. As in the case of Alberto Caeiro, however, the general affinity between Campos and Whitman should not blind us to the fact that the two poets are also different. Whitman wrote utopian poems about such things as railroad engines and steamships. Campos also writes about machines, but his verse is more violent and Marinetti-like in its dynamic ferocity. He is always "grinding his teeth" and feverishly extolling the tough "eternal r-r-r-r" of the modern mechanical age (1:878). Like Whitman, Campos is a homoerotic poet; but he also shares this tendency with Pessoa "himself," who had already composed two lengthy homoerotic poems in English.[5] Moreover, Campos's sexual passages have a different tone from Whitman's—as in "Ode Triunfal," where the speaker becomes positively orgasmic as he ponders the deadly arsenal of futurist technology:

Eh, cimento armado, beton de cimento, novos processos!
Progressos dos armamentos gloriosamente mortíferos!
Couraças, canhões, metralhadoras, submarinos, aeroplanos!

Amo-vos a todos, a tudo, como uma fera.
Amo-vos carnivoramente,
Pervertidamente e enroscando a minha vista
Em vós, ó coisas grandes, banais, úteis, inúteis,

Ó coisas todas modernas,
Ó minhas contemporâneas, forma actual e próxima
Do sistema imediato do Universo!
Nova Revelação metálica e dinâmica de Deus! (1:881)

[Hey, armed cement, cement mixer, new processes!
Progress of gloriously deadly armaments!
Armor-plate, cannons, machine guns, submarines, airplanes!

I love you, I love everything like a wild animal.
I love you carnivorously,
Pervertedly, coiling my sight
Round you, oh large, banal, useful and useless things,
Oh all modern things,
Oh my contemporaries, present and future form
Of the immediate system of the Universe!
New, metallic and dynamic Revelation of God!]

Campos is less benign, more *noir*-ish than Whitman; he anticipates a figure like Hart Crane, and his sexuality is overtly masochistic. For example, he nearly swoons at the thought of being caught up in the teeth of moving gears; and at one point, he gushes about his desire to experience what Victorian writers called "the English vice": "Espanquem-me a bordo de navios!" [Spank me on board ships] (1:882).

Both Pessoa "himself" and Campos are strongly attracted to the sea, which they associate with Portugal's great period of empire. For both, the sea has an oneiric power, enabling the poet to travel into the past or to experience visions of the future. In *Mensagem*, Pessoa uses this "dreamy" quality to review the victories and defeats of Portugal's "Golden Age" of discoveries and to assess the country's potential return to its former greatness. In "Ode Marítima," however, Campos seems to experience the sea voyage as a kind of infinite wet dream. Once he leaves the restricting shores of civilization, his language immediately becomes excited and sensuous: "Toda a vida marítima! tudo na vida marítima! / Insinua-se no meu sangue toda essa sedução fina / E eu cismo indeterminadamente as viagens" [All maritime life, everything in maritime life! / All this fine seduction insinuates itself in my blood / And I become indeterminately obsessed with voyages] (1:895). Even the *volante*, or ship's fly-wheel, becomes a sexual image:

Toma-me pouco a pouco o delírio das coisas marítimas,
Penetram-me fisicamente o cais e a sua atmosfera,

O marulho do Tejo galga-me por cima dos sentidos,
E começo a sonhar, começo a envolver-me do sonho das águas,
Começam a pegar bem as correias-de-transmissão na minh'alma
E a aceleração do volante sacode-me nitidamente. (1:897)

[The delirium of maritime things overcomes me little by little,
The dock and its atmosphere penetrate me physically,
The tossing of the Tagus leaps over my senses,
And I begin to dream, I begin to wrap myself in the dream of
    waters,
The transmission chains begin to grab hard on my soul
And the acceleration of the fly-wheel openly shakes me.]

The furious shaking of the fly-wheel opens the way to the darker, more sexually explicit aspects of the dream-voyage, which involve an encounter with pirates. As recent studies of the history of sexuality have shown, pirates have long been associated with the idea of sodomy and with homoerotic fantasy.[6] "Ode Marítima" makes this association explicit, first by dreaming its way into a nightmarish past:

Os piratas, a pirataria, os barcos, a hora,
Aquela hora marítima em que as presas são assaltadas,
E o terror dos apresados foge pra loucura—essa hora,
No seu total de crimes, terror, barcos, gente, mar, céu, nuvens,
Brisa, latitude, longitude, vozearia,
Queria eu que fosse em seu Todo meu corpo em seu Todo,
    sofrendo . . . (1:905)

[The pirates, the piracy, the boats, the hour,
That maritime hour when the prisoners are assaulted,
And the terror of those seized becomes madness—that hour,
In all its crimes, terror, boats, people, sea, sky, clouds,
Breeze, latitude, longitude, voices in uproar,
I wish that this Totality were my body in its Totality, suffering . . .]

Soon, the poet is experiencing a fantasy of torture and rape by piratical "rough trade":

Ó meus peludos e rudes heróis da aventura e do crime!
Minhas marítimas feras, maridos da minha imaginação!
Amantes casuais da obliquidade das minhas sensações!
Queria ser Aquela que vos esperasse nos portos,

A vós, odiados amados do seu sangue de pirata nos sonhos! (1:906)
. . .
O bárbaros do antigo mar!
Rasgai-me e feri-me!
De leste a oeste do meu corpo
Riscai de sangue a minha carne! (1:908)
. . .
Fazei de mim qualquer coisa como se eu fosse
Arrastado—ó prazer, ó beijada dor!—
Arrastado à cauda de cavalos chicoteados por vós . . .
Mas isto no mar, isto no ma-a-ar, isto no MA-A-A-AR!
Eh-eh-eh-eh-eh! Eh-eh-eh-eh-eh-eh-eh! EH-EH-EH-EH-
    EH-EH-EH! No MA-A-A-A-AR! (1:909)

[Oh, my rough and hairy heroes of adventure and crime!
My maritime beasts, husbands of my imagination!
Casual lovers of the obliquity of my sensations!
I wanted to be She who waited for you on the docks,
For you, hateful lovers, with your pirate blood in dreams!
. . .
Oh barbarians of the ancient sea!
Rip me open, wound me!
Mark from east to west
The flesh of my body with blood!
. . .
Make of me anything as if I were
A wretch—oh pleasure, oh kissed pain!—
Dragged by the tail of horses whipped by you . . .
But on the sea, on the sea, on the SE-A-A-A-A!
Ha-ha-ha-ha-ha! Ha-ha-ha-ha-ha-ha-ha! HA-HA-HA-HA-
    HA-HA-HA! On the SE-A-A-A-A!]

This is Whitman transformed by Marinetti's "words at liberty," and by
Campos's fantasy of a crazed sadomasochistic orgy on the open seas. Like
Whitman, Campos enthralls the reader with his expansive and passionate
rhetoric, but his images are bizarre and violent, and even his rather campy
sexual exuberance tends to be undercut by the delirious tone of his laughter.

    There is a similar emphasis on homosexuality in "Saudação a Walt
Whitman," where Campos hails the American poet as his "brother in the
Universe":

Ó sempre moderno e eterno, cantor dos concretos absolutos,
Concubina fogosa do universo disperso,
Grande pederasta roçando-te contra a adversidade das coisas,
Sexualizado pelas pedras, pelas árvores, pelas pessoas, pelas
    profissões,
Cio das passagens, dos encontros casuais, das meras
    observações . . .

               . . .

Quantas vezes eu beijo o teu retrato!
Lá onde estás agora (não sei onde é mas é Deus)
Sentes isto, sei que o sentes, e os meus beijos são mais quentes (em
    gente)
E tu assim é que os queres, meu velho, e agradeces de lá—,
Sei-o bem, qualquer coisa mo diz, um agrado no meu espírito

Uma erecção abstracta e indirecta no fundo da minha alma.

Nada do *engageant* em ti, mas ciclópico e musculoso,
Mas perante o Universo a tua atitude era de mulher,
E cada erva, cada pedra, cada homem era para ti o Universo.
(1:922–23)

[Oh, always modern and eternal, singer of concrete absolutes,
Fiery concubine of the universe dispersed,
Great pederast rubbing against the adversity of things,
Sexualized by rocks, by trees, by persons, by professions,
Heat from crossings, from casual encounters, from mere
    observations . . .

               . . .

How many times I kiss your picture!
There where you are now (I don't know where that is but it is God)
You feel this, I know you feel it, and my kisses are hotter (in
    person)
And you like them that way, my dear old fellow, and you give
    thanks from there—,
I know it well, something tells it to me, a delight in my spirit

An abstract and indirect erection in the depth of my soul.

Nothing of the *engageant* in you, rather cyclopean and muscular,
But before the Universe your attitude was of a woman,

And each blade of grass, each rock, each man was the Universe for
you.]

Until this point, the "Saudação" is an effective commentary on Whitman, written in a language that seems to catch the spirit of his poetry. Soon
after, however, Campos drifts into an erotic hallucination involving machines, handcuffs, and rough sailors:

Clímax a ferro e motores!
Escadaria pela velocidade acima, sem degraus!
Bomba hidráulica desancorando-me as entranhas sentidas!

Ponham-me grilhetas só para eu as partir!
Só para eu as partir com os dentes, e que os dentes sangrem
Gozo masoquista, espasmódico a sangue, da vida!

Os marinheiros levaram-me preso,
As mãos apertaram-me no escuro,
Morri temporariamente de senti-lo,
Seguiu-se a minh'alma a lamber o chão do cárcere privado,
E a cega-rega das impossibilidades contornando o meu acinte.
(1:926–27)

[Climax of iron and motors!
Stairway above through velocity, without stairs!
Hydraulic bomb weighing the anchor of my sorry bowels!

Put the shackles on me just so I can break them!
Just so I can break them with my teeth, and so my teeth may bleed
A masochistic, spasmodic joy of life in blood!

The sailors took me prisoner,
Their hands closed tightly upon me in the dark,
I temporarily died from feeling it,
My soul proceeded to lick the ground of the private cell,
And the cicada-like sound of impossibilities surrounding my
spiteful taunt.]

The poem ends on a bittersweet note with the poet's realization that, unlike
the "Great Liberator," he lacks both a utopian mission and Whitman's
"calma superior a [s]i próprio" [superior calm over (him)self] (1:928). The
last phrase evokes Campos's "master," Caeiro, who epitomizes the tranquil

poet. But in a more general sense, it expresses a certain fear of uncontrolled subjectivity which we can deduce from all of Pessoa's heteronyms.

Campos's unleashed passion (often bordering on what Pessoa "himself" regarded as the "obscene") constitutes the "romantic" face of his modernism. Like the proto-Freudians of the nineteenth century, he is an addict who drinks and smokes and who, when he is not suffering from insomnia, loves to experience dreams and hallucinations. Certain lines from two poems written toward the end of his radical phase sound like Shelley's "To Night," in which the suffering poet beseeches the darkness: "Come soon, soon!" In "Passagem das Horas" [Passage of the hours], Campos makes a similar plea: "Vem, ó noite, e apaga-me, vem e afoga-me em ti" [Come, O night, and extinguish me, come and drown me in you] (1:932); and in "Dois Excertos de Odes" [Two excerpts from odes], he cries: "Vem, Noite, antiquíssima e idêntica . . . / Vem e arranca-me / Do solo de angústia e de inutilidade / Onde vicejo" [Come, Night, so very ancient and the same . . . / Come and pull me / From the soil of anguish and uselessness / Where I luxuriate] (1:886–87).

After 1916, Campos's poetry shifts away from the frenetic modernist experimentation of his odes and assumes a more subdued tone, as if the flywheel of his dreams were no longer spinning. The sea imagery subsides, and his verses put greater emphasis on city scenes. The sexual euphoria also recedes, replaced by a kind of somber detumescence, although the poet is far from serene. He even becomes reconciled to earlier styles of poetry; scattered through his late, predominantly free-verse poems are a few sonnets and other traditional forms.

Although the theme of death is apparent in Campos's earlier poems, it becomes a primary issue after 1916. In dealing with this theme, however, he usually keeps his somewhat irreverent sense of humor. A good example is "Soneto Já Antigo" [Now ancient sonnet], in which the poet, addressing a woman, speaks of his own death. Conceptually and stylistically, the poem calls to mind certain odes by Reis, where a neoclassical shepherdess/muse becomes the sounding board for the poet's prediction of his eventual death. But in contrast to Reis, Campos is mock-heroic. "Olha, Daisy" [Look here, Daisy], he begins, as if he were speaking to a commoner rather than a goddess. He tells "Daisy" that when he dies, she should go straight to his London friends and grieve over his death—even though she, of course, won't feel anything. Then she should travel to York and break the news to one of his other lovers, a "pobre rapazito / que me deu tantas horas tão felizes" [poor little fellow / who gave me so many happy hours]. While she is at it, she should also inform "essa estranha Cecily / que acreditava que eu

seria grande . . ." [that strange Cecily / who thought I would be great].
Finally, he ends the poem with a curse: "Raios partam a vida e quem lá
ande!" [Damn life to hell and those in it!] (1:951).

A more profound cynicism can be heard in a longer, untitled work about
death and its effects on friends and loved ones. Here it is unclear whether
Campos is talking to himself or to someone else; in either case, he doesn't
mince words: "Se te queres matar, por que não te queres matar?" [If you
want to kill yourself, why don't you?] (1:953). He then proceeds to dismiss
every reason for not committing suicide:

> A mágoa dos outros? . . . Tens remorso adiantado
> De que te chorem?
> Descansa: pouco te chorarão . . .
> O impulso vital apaga as lágrimas pouco a pouco,
> Quando não são de coisas nossas,
> Quando são do que acontece aos outros, sobretudo a morte,
> Porque é coisa depois da qual nada acontece aos outros . . . (1:953)

> [Others' grief? . . . You feel remorseful because you think
> That they'll cry for you?
> Relax: they'll cry little for you . . .
> The urge to live extinguishes tears little by little,
> When they're not about our own things,
> When they're about what happens to others, especially death,
> Because nothing happens to others after that . . .]

Campos's sense of personal failure and existential despair is given its
most complex expression in "Tabacaria" [Tobacco Shop]—a long, free-
verse poem that dramatizes his fragile hold on his own identity. I shall not
attempt to explicate this poem, which has been the subject of countless
new-critical readings; but I do want to emphasize how its themes are connected to the central preoccupations of all the major heteronyms.[7] The
initial lines of the poem seem to echo both Reis and Pessoa "himself" when
they approach the emotional depths: "Não sou nada. / Nunca serei nada. /
Não posso querer ser nada" [I'm nothing. / I'll always be nothing. / Even
wishing, I'll still be nothing] (1:960). Given the fact that Campos is only
one of many heteronyms, the first-person pronoun in these lines has a special ambiguity. Indeed, the poem as a whole can be read in at least three
senses. On the "realist" level, it orchestrates the shifting moods of a lonely,
depressed, middle-aged man rather like Pessoa himself. On the metalin-
guistic level, it reveals the process whereby the heteronyms transform

"nothing" into lyric verse. And on the level of the poet named Campos, it shows how a propensity for romantic dreaming can offer consolation for despair. Hence Campos's nihilism is immediately canceled out by a contradictory or paradoxical statement: "À parte isso, tenho em mim todos os sonhos do mundo" [Aside from this, I have all the dreams of the world in me]. "Nothingness" is reduced to a mere grammatical shifter *(isso)*, and the "I" of the poem now contains limitless possibilities.

This contradictory emotional movement can be found in nearly everything that Campos wrote, particularly in works like "Ode Triunfal" and "Ode Marítima," in which a lonely engineer standing on the dock gradually dreams himself onto the high seas. In "Tabacaria," the transition between quotidian depression and imaginative power is represented in a more direct and sober fashion through the poet's voyeuristic observations of the world outside his window, especially the movement around the tobacco shop across the street.

The sense of emotional tension in the poem arises out of an elementary opposition posed by Campos's "master," Caeiro, between the "real" and the "metaphysical" worlds. There is never any question about which side of these realms Caeiro prefers. As he tells us in the first line of his poem "V": "Há metafísica bastante em não pensar em nada" [There's enough metaphysics in not thinking about anything].[8] The slightly more contemplative figure, Reis, follows Caeiro's advice, disciplining himself never to succumb totally to "metaphysics" and to calmly accept the inevitability of death. By contrast, Campos is the self-conscious and fantastic poet par excellence. What interests him most is not the everyday world but the dream; not the object itself, but the mystery it conceals. He is the kind of writer whom Caeiro finds irritating—the "mystic" who sees sermons in stones and is forever dissatisfied and questioning. As he himself says in "Tabacaria," he never does anything but dream:

> Tenho sonhado mais que o que Napoleão fez.
> Tenho apertado ao peito hipotético mais humanidades do que
>   Cristo,
> Tenho feito filosofias em segredo que nenhum Kant escreveu.
> Mas sou, e talvez serei sempre, o da mansarda,
> Ainda que não more nela;
> Serei sempre o *que não nasceu para isso;*
> Serei sempre só o *que tinha qualidade;*
> Serei sempre o que esperou que lhe abrissem a porta ao pé de uma
>   parede sem porta,

E cantou a cantiga do Infinito numa capoeira,
E ouviu a voz de Deus num poço tapado.
Crer em mim? Não, nem em nada. (1:962)

[I've dreamed more than what Napoleon ever did.
I've pressed to my hypothetical chest more humanities than Christ,
I've secretly made philosophies that no Kant ever wrote.
But I am, and perhaps will forever be, the one in the attic,
Even though I don't live in one;
I'll forever be *the one who was not born for this;*
I'll forever be merely *the one who had qualities;*
I'll forever be the one who waited for them to open the door close
    to a wall without a door,
And sang a song about the Infinite in a chicken coop,
And heard the voice of God in a sealed well.
Believe in myself? No, nor in anything.]

Although he is a dreamer, Campos is also, at times like this, an even greater skeptic than Caeiro or Reis. For him, neither the object nor the subject exists—both are forms of dreamy idealism. But as Campos sits in his chair and smokes cigarettes, he becomes imaginatively engaged with what he regards as true life across the street:

(Come chocolates, pequena;
Come chocolates!
Olha que não há mais metafísica no mundo senão chocolates.

Pudesse eu comer chocolates com a mesma verdade com que
    comes!
Mas eu penso e, ao tirar o papel de prata, que é de folha de
    estanho,
Deito tudo para o chão, como tenho deitado a vida.) (1:962–63)

[(Eat chocolates, little girl;
Eat chocolates!
Look, there's nothing more metaphysical in the world than
    chocolates.

Would that I could eat chocolates with the same truth with which
    you eat!
But I think, and upon removing the silver paper, the tinfoil,
I let everything drop to the ground, just as I have dropped my life.)]

Here Campos sounds like Pessoa "himself" in the famous poem on the reaper, which I discussed in chapter 3. In one sense, the only difference between the two poems is that "Tabacaria" involves a speaker in an urban setting who observes a young girl un-self-consciously eating chocolates. Like Pessoa "himself," Campos wants to experience the girl's enjoyment. "Tabacaria" could therefore be read as "The Reaper" translated into an ironic mode. The only things that keep the poet from total despair are the sight of people across the street and the taste of cigarettes: "Enquanto o Destino mo conceder, continuarei fumando" [As long as Destiny allows me, I'll continue smoking] (1:965). As befits this irony, the poem ends on a wryly humorous note. From the window, Campos sees a man leaving the tobacco shop; he identifies him as "Esteves sem metafísica" [Esteves without metaphysics]. The man unexpectedly turns and waves good-bye to the poet, as if he were aware of their common destiny. Shocked, the poet shouts back, "*Adeus ó Esteves*," as the tobacco shop owner looks on and smiles openly.

The later poems in Campos's collection tend to repeat this same pattern: the tedium and anguish of existence, the poet's failed hopes, and the imminence of death are all turned into a verse that hovers nicely between despair and ironic wit. In "Insónia" [Insomnia], Campos uses an image identical to the "living corpse" in poems by Reis and Pessoa "himself": "Não durmo, jazo, cadáver acordado, sentindo, / E meu sentimento é um pensamento vazio" [I don't sleep, I recline, awakened cadaver, sentient, / Feeling an empty thought] (1:978). But just when Campos seems at his lowest, he writes a poem like "Bicarbonato de Soda" [Bicarbonate of soda], in which he affirms a desire to live:

> Súbita, uma angústia . . .
> Ah, que angústia, que náusea do estômago à alma!
> Que amigos que tenho tido!
> Que vazias de tudo as cidades que tenho percorrido!
> Que esterco metafísico os meus propósitos todos!
>
> Devo tomar qualquer coisa ou suicidar-me?
> Não: vou existir. Arre! Vou existir!
> E-xis-tir . . .
> E-xis-tir . . . (1:987)

> [Suddenly, a pain . . .
> Ah, what pain, what stomach nausea to the soul!
> What friends I have had!

How empty of everything the cities I have traversed!
What metaphysical manure all my intentions!

Should I take something or kill myself?
No: I'm going to live. Dammit! I'm going to live!
L-i-ve . . .
L-i-ve . . .]

This turnabout technique originates not with Campos but with the youthful Pessoa, who parodied some of his own melancholic poems such as "Quando Ela Passa" and who often treated the same themes in different modes or styles. As I have tried to suggest in this chapter and elsewhere and as other critics have noted, the differences between Campos and the other heteronyms, or among the heteronyms themselves, are ultimately less important than the structural similarities among them, which allow Pessoa to work variations on two or three basic themes. Pessoa once commented that it was difficult to simulate the differences among his heteronyms whenever they wrote in prose, adding that: "[a] simulação é mais fácil, até porque é mais espontânea, em verso" [simulation is easier in verse if only because it's more spontaneous] (2:344). Not surprisingly, critical studies have tended to concentrate on the distinct characters of the various poets—as if anything that they had in common might diminish the project as a whole. But the importance of Pessoa's heteronyms has less to do with issues of originality or uniqueness than with stylistic variations on several elementary constants. Without exception, all of Pessoa's heteronyms are preoccupied with large, existential problems: the meaning of life, the inevitability of death, and the conflict between the rational and emotional sides of human nature. Likewise, all of the heteronyms are preoccupied with the cultural history of Portugal and its place within the larger continent of Europe. In the final analysis, their "individuality" can be seen in their different stylistic responses to concerns they all share. Out of his knowledge, imagination, and expertise, Pessoa was able to create a group of contemporary poets who have different filiations with Portuguese, Anglo-American, and European literary history. His greatest achievement was not simply the idea of the heteronyms but the way he managed to weave different traditions or poetic ideologies into an array of personae who, at bottom, were remarkably alike.

Text Versus Work

Constructing and Deconstructing a National Poet

As we have seen, Pessoa wrote in many voices, challenging the notion of coherent identity. The irony is that since his death he has become an "author"—an ostensibly coherent personality who is discussed as if all the contradictions and inconsistencies of his writings were products of a master plan. Every editor, translator, and critic who has worked on Pessoa has tended to project a kind of metapersonality onto his diverse manuscripts, thereby turning him into a godlike figure who controlled a sort of puppet show of various personae or styles. In this chapter, I want to challenge directly the idea that we can ever arrive at an authoritative picture of Pessoa. I do not want to deny that he was an actual, historical subject who had ideas about politics, religion, and poetry; but I do want to problematize his agency, or to show how it has been mediated by various historical factors. The history of Pessoa scholarship reveals quite clearly that Pessoa the author is a less stable figure than we might imagine and that his images have been constructed posthumously, sometimes in order to serve nationalist agendas and ideological needs.

The canonization of Pessoa began in the late 1920s, when, somewhat like the disciples of Alberto Caeiro, a younger generation of Portuguese modernists discovered in him a "master" and began the formal discussion and dissemination of his work in their literary review, *Presença* (1927–1940). One of leaders of this group was the poet José Régio, whose influential essay, "Literatura Viva" [Live literature] (1927) ranked Pessoa alongside Camões and Gil Vicente, two of Portugal's most-revered writers.[1] Other Pessoa enthusiasts included João Gaspar Simões and Adolfo Casais Monteiro, who carried out an extensive correspondence with the poet. Pessoa's written responses to these two men are crucial to any critical discussion of his work and are the chief means by which he explained his artistic intentions; indeed, they are less like casual letters than like a formal discourse, addressed to an audience of critics who would eventually serve as Pessoa's commentators.

At the end of his life, Pessoa was recognized as a great author within Portugal's small literary community, but to the world beyond he was relatively unknown. The writer Miguel Torga lamented this fact in his diary: "*3 de Dezembro*—Morreu Fernando Pessoa. Mal acabei de ler a notícia no jornal, fechei a porta do consultório e meti-me pelos montes a cabo. Fui chorar com os pinheiros e com as fragas a morte do nosso maior poeta de hoje, que Portugal viu passar num caixão para a eternidade sem ao menos perguntar quem era" [*3rd of December*—Fernando Pessoa died. I barely finished reading the notice in the newspaper, when I closed the door of my office and took refuge deep in the mountains. Amidst the pine trees and bluffs, I wept the death of our greatest poet today, whom Portugal saw pass by for all eternity in a coffin, without even asking who he was] (3:1375).

Pessoa's longtime friend Luís de Montalvor voiced a somewhat similar theme in the obituary that he wrote for the "Grande Poeta de Portugal" [Great poet of Portugal] in the *Diário de Notícias*. Like Torga, Montalvor emphasized Pessoa's anonymity or romantic obscurity, thereby heightening his appeal to the cognoscenti; after summarizing the poet's achievements, Montalvor concluded with a solemn yet tender appeal to readers: "Quem o quiser compreender folheie a sua obra vasta e dispersa. Começará a amá-lo" [Whoever wishes to understand him should leaf through his vast and scattered work. You will begin to love him] (3:1415).

Few if any of Pessoa's friends claimed actually to understand this eccentric and very private man, who had died from drink; nor did they realize at the time just how "vast and scattered" his work had become. Soon after his death in 1935, more than twenty-five thousand of the unpublished items he had written were discovered in an old trunk in his apartment, providing rich material for the construction of an authorial career. Montalvor and Simões began to organize and edit this material at the request of Pessoa's family; and in July 1936, the editorial group at *Presença* published a commemorative issue on Pessoa, in which they pledged "nunca deixar de se ocupar do grande poeta. Será mais um modo de se afirmar fiel à missão, de que não desiste, de proclamar e defender quaisquer valores espirituais em geral, estéticos em particular, contra todas as antipatias violentas mas impotentes que se lhes opõem" [never to stop working on behalf of the great poet. It will be one more way of (*Presença*'s) affirming itself faithful to the mission, toward which it remains firm, of proclaiming and defending any spiritual values in general, aesthetic in particular, against all violent but

presença

fôlha de arte e crítica
coimbra, julho, 1936

É ste número consagrado a Fernando Pessoa, em quem «presença» se orgulha de ter reconhecido sempre uma das mais ricas e originais individualidades da literatura portuguesa. Não podendo ser o que sonharíamos fôsse, (é bom sempre sonhar mais!) nem sendo a personalidade de Fernando Pessoa para caber quer num número de revista quer num volume ou cento de volumes, «presença» promete nunca deixar de se ocupar do grande poeta. Será mais um modo de se afirmar fiel à missão, de que não desiste, de proclamar e defender quaisquer valores espirituais em geral, estéticos em particular, contra tôdas as antipatias violentas mas impotentes que se lhes opõem.

ano décimo 48 volume segundo

The cover of *Presença*'s commemorative issue on Pessoa, July 1936.

impotent antipathies that oppose them].[2] The language here is very much in keeping with the high-modernist values of *Presença*, which was vaguely *symboliste* in tone, devoted to a "spiritual" and "artistic" mission. In the process of creating a memorial image of Pessoa, *Presença* tended to emphasize the aestheticized qualities of his writing, meanwhile portraying him as a hero of art who stood firm against his "impotent" political or cultural enemies. Exactly who these enemies might be is not clear, but it seems obvious that Pessoa was being claimed on behalf of a particular ideology in opposition to a hyposticized Other, which was defined as secular and insufficiently appreciative of the highest artistic values.[3]

Sorting and organizing Pessoa's writings was clearly a formidable task. His trunk contained manuscripts for nonfiction books, essays, plays, poetry, and every imaginable genre. In addition to a great deal of material in more-or-less completed form, there were fragments of prose and poetry, unsigned and undated manuscripts, and many handwritten documents that were virtually illegible. What the prospective editors were faced with was an unbounded, unstructured discourse, in some ways resembling Pessoa's other writings but not yet shaped into published form. In other words, they were looking at what Roland Barthes has described as a "text," or at the pure activity of writing before it has been packaged, commodified, and turned into an object that can be placed on a shelf.

As Barthes explains it, "the text is that *social* space that leaves no language safe, outside, nor any subject of the enunciation in position as judge, master, analyst, confessor, decoder." The text has no metalanguage to determine its meaning, no author who gives it an aura of stability. Pessoa's editors (like editors everywhere) attempted to change this situation, converting an unstable social activity into its opposite, which Barthes calls the "work." Barthes elaborates the difference between the two terms as follows: "[T]he work is a fragment of substance, occupying a part of the space of books (in a library for example), the Text is a methodological field . . . [T]he work can be seen (in bookshops, in catalogues, in exam syllabuses), the text is a process of demonstration, speaks according to certain rules (or against certain rules); the work can be held in the hand, the text is held in language."[4]

Interestingly, in the preface to the first volume of their edition of Pessoa's collected writings, Montalvor and Simões use the term "work" in exactly the way Barthes means it, but they seem unaware of its potential ideological implication:

Na verdade, não estávamos perante o caso vulgar do escritor que, tendo dado à estampa, em vida, o melhor do seu génio, nos lega, à hora da morte, alguns manuscritos no fundo de uma gaveta. Não. O caso de Fernando Pessoa é diferente: ao morrer, este poeta estava por assim dizer inédito. Tudo quanto dele nos ficou por publicar, a par do que deixou disperso em revistas, constitui a *sua obra. A sua obra* ficará sendo aquela que *post-mortem* os seus leitores venham a conhecer. Isto é: a sua obra ficará sendo esta mesma que ora publicamos. Eis por que julgamos de nosso dever apenas dar à estampa nestes definitivos volumes das suas obras completas aquilo que de certo modo o próprio poeta já consideraria definitivo. Uma vez publicados os volumes relativos a cada um dos heterónimos . . . nada obstará então a que se reúnam num volume só todas aquelas composições que pela natureza fragmentária ou inacabada factura seriam descabidas nos volumes das suas obras definitivas.[5]

[In truth we were not facing the usual case of a writer who, having published the best of his genius during his lifetime, bequeathed to us at the hour of his death some manuscripts in the bottom of a drawer. No. The case of Fernando Pessoa is different: when this poet died, he was, generally speaking, unpublished. Everything that was left for us to publish, along with what was scattered in magazines, constitutes *his work. His work* will be that which *post-mortem* his readers will come to know. That is, his work will be that which we are now publishing. This is why we believe our task was merely to publish in these definitive volumes of his complete works the writings which in a sense the poet himself had already considered definitive. Once the volumes pertaining to each of the heteronyms are published . . . then nothing will hinder the gathering into a single volume of all those compositions which, because of their fragmentary or incomplete nature, would be unsuitable for the volumes of his definitive works.]

Notice how this conversion of text into work involves an appeal to an idea of an author—a sort of ideal Pessoa who stands in a mysterious a priori relation to the book we are reading, providing a metalanguage that enables the editors to distinguish some writings from others. Hence the "definitive" volumes of [Pessoa's] complete works are defined somewhat vaguely, as those writings which "in a sense" Pessoa himself had "already considered definitive." But which Pessoa are the editors talking about? Given his many heteronyms, the problem of establishing a transcendent subjectivity or simple intention is especially vexing.

What the editors did not comprehend when this preface was published in 1942 was the sheer amount of "unsuitable" material in Pessoa's trunk. A significant portion of Pessoa's "work" is in fact highly insubstantial, threatening the coherence of the metalanguage constructed around it.[6] To limit the amount of problematic material, the editors took a special approach to the numerous poems that lacked a signature: instead of placing them together in a separate volume, they assigned each one an author, based on a stylistic comparison with poems signed by Pessoa and the other heteronyms. In other words, they combined unsigned verse with signed verse to make up the "definitive" work of the various heteronyms. In their attempt to force a certain logic on this material, they claimed they were "naturalmente" [naturally] attributing authorship to the unsigned poems and were assuming that "pouco deve[m] ter errado nessas atribuições" [(they) should have erred little in these attributions].[7] It seems obvious, however, that they were taking certain liberties. Pessoa was known to change his mind from time to time about which of his heteronyms had written what; and although he outlined a number of ideas for the publication of his works, he left no definitive plan.[8]

Published by Ática in Lisbon, the "definitive" volumes of Pessoa's poetry took over thirty years to complete. (The eleventh and final volume appeared the year of the Portuguese revolution; eight years later, in 1982, the ninth and last volume of a prose series was completed.) At the beginning of the project, Montalvor and Simões were optimistic that they could finish by 1943, but they cautioned that their edition might take time: "Quando se trabalha com cuidado é preciso trabalhar devagar. Fernando Pessoa merece-o. Quanto ao tempo, tempo não faltará, pois não é de um poeta da hora presente que se trata, mas de um poeta da Eternidade" [When one works carefully, it is necessary to work slowly. Fernando Pessoa deserves it. As for time, there will be no lack of time, for this is not about a poet of the present hour, but rather a poet of Eternity].[9] As they wrote these lines, Montalvor and Simões were well aware that other volumes of Pessoa's writing were beginning to appear; for example, Adolfo Casais Monteiro published a two-volume collection of Pessoa's previously published poems in 1942, the same year that the first Ática volume was released. Not surprisingly, as new editions and anthologies multiplied, there were scholarly debates over ascriptions and transcriptions. In a preface to the third volume in the Ática collection, Montalvor and Simões seemed already on the defensive and felt the need to elaborate on their initial editorial statement. They now admitted that their editorial strategy was "talvez não isenta de erro" [perhaps not free of error], but they resented any suggestion that they were setting themselves up as "censores infalíveis" [infallible censors].[10] The arguments became more heated as the years passed. The struggle for control over Pessoa was at times so intense that even longtime friends became antagonists. This was the case of Jacinto do Prado Coelho and George Rudolf Lind, who quarreled over the organization of the *Livro do Desassossego*.[11]

Among Pessoa's "disciples," Simões seemed especially determined to fulfill the *presencista* pledge of loyalty to the "Great Poet." In 1950, his massive, six-hundred-page biography of Pessoa appeared, which he described as an *explicação*, even though he was careful to say that the "definitive" account had yet to be written. Despite its often rapturous adulation of Pessoa and its sometimes vulgar Freudianism, this biography remains the best and most comprehensive discussion of Pessoa's life and works. Along with the early writings of Casais Monteiro and Coelho, it laid the groundwork for future critical studies on the poet.

It should be recalled that both the biography and the pioneer editing of Pessoa's work occurred during the Estado Novo (1933–1974), when censorship committees routinely scrutinized and suppressed all materials that were considered subversive. Interestingly, the business of publishing and commenting on Pessoa seems to have gone on unobstructed, despite the homoerotic elements in certain of his poems. The censors may simply have overlooked this aspect of his writing, which was limited to a few references or motifs scattered through long and difficult poems, or they may have missed certain implications that seem clear to us in retrospect. At that time, Pessoa was known as the respected, patriotic author of *Mensagem*, a book whose nationalism had been rewarded by the regime. Indeed the most explicitly political material that he had published was a 1928 manifesto, entitled *O Interregno: Defesa e Justificação do Regime Militar em Portugal* [The interregnum: Defense and justification of the military regime in Portugal], which expressed his hope for "a salvação e renascimento do País" [the salvation and rebirth of the country] (3:795).

It is by no means clear that Pessoa would have supported the Estado Novo had he lived beyond its initial phase. Shortly before his death, he composed a few short poems that indicate his dissatisfaction with the dictatorship. In one of these, entitled "Sim, é o Estado Novo" [Yes, it's the Estado Novo], he comments on the mediocrity of the regime and the corruption of the *padres* [priests] and *doutores* [academics] who occupied positions of power. His attack on clerics and teachers strikes close to Salazar himself, who, prior to his political rise, was a Catholic economics professor at the University of Coimbra. In another poem, entitled "António de Oliveira Salazar," Pessoa's criticism becomes even more personal, targeting the dictator's much publicized "saintly" asceticism:

Mas enfim é
Certo e certeiro
Que isto consola
E nos dá fé.
Que o coitadinho
Do tiraninho
Não bebe vinho,
Nem até
Café. (1:579)

[But finally it is
Right and mete
That this console
And give us faith.
For the poor little
Fellow of a tyrant
Drinks neither wine
Nor even
Caffeine.]

Some critics have regarded these poems as proof of Pessoa's antireactionary attitude once the Estado Novo got underway. Ultimately, however, Pessoa's exact political position is unclear. Just as his enthusiasm for the Republic waned in the years following its inception, he seems to have become disenchanted with Salazar. The Republican years had been turbulent, with governments changing regularly. During the period, Pessoa/Campos published a ridiculing note about President Afonso Costa's near-fatal fall from a cable car, as if his unsteady footing were symbolic of the clumsiness and instability of the Republic as a whole. The Salazar regime offered a much greater sense of continuity, but Salazar lacked the charisma of other European dictators such as Hitler, Mussolini, or Pessoa's beloved but fallen "President-King" Sidónio Pais. Salazar preferred somber clothes and an unassuming lifestyle to military uniforms and parades; he was, in historian Tom Gallagher's words, "a dictator of the sacristy rather than of the balcony,"[12] and this priestly image annoyed the anti-Catholic Pessoa. Equally important where Pessoa was concerned, the regime's austere economic policies and isolationist attitude made Portugal seem more provincial while other European nations were undergoing rapid modernization.

Salazar was more interested in nostalgia and religion than in industrialization and progress. In pursuit of these ideals, one of his major cultural achievements was to elevate Camões, the chronicler of the "Age of Discoveries" to the status of national hero. As critic Irwin Stern has observed, the government treated Camões's birthday as a national holiday, and pilgrimages were made to his grave in the Jerónimos, a major national monument. A film about Camões's "sacrifices" was produced during World War II to boost public morale, and an even more intensive program of celebrations got underway once the wars for independence in Africa began.[13] Busts and statues of the poet were placed in parks, and his figure was chiseled alongside those of Vasco da Gama and other famous navigators on a huge monument to Prince Henry the Navigator and overseas expansion, which was built by Salazar in 1940 on the shores of the Tagus.

As Gallagher has noted, because of Salazar's desire to "revive the old and resist the new," the country never experienced the right-wing cultural revolution that took place in Germany and Italy.[14] For his part, Pessoa had wanted to usher in just such a cultural revolution, which would change the course of Portuguese letters. He was also convinced that in order for this revolution to occur, Portugal needed to industrialize and take its place alongside other modern West European nations.[15] In other words, his criticism of Salazar was not necessarily left-wing or antireactionary. On this score, he was more in tune with the "revolutionary classicism" of high-modernist thinking in the 1920s and 1930s, and his association with the newspaper *Revolução* [Revolution] in 1932 and 1933 suggests a possible shift in his sympathies to the far right.

The editor of *Revolução* was Francisco Rolão Preto, one of the founders of Portuguese integralism (1914), who supported the military regime until Salazar was named premier in 1932. That same year, Preto formed the national syndicalism movement and its "Camisas Azuis" [Blue Shirts], with the idea of challenging Salazar, whom he regarded as a political lightweight. Pessoa's change of attitude toward Salazar between 1928 and 1935 might be understood as indirect support for Preto, who was an extremely popular and charismatic leader.[16] At the very least, Pessoa openly associated himself with *Revolução*, which published an excerpt from his *Livro do Desassossego* and the twelve-poem series entitled "Mar Português."

Salazar finally outlawed the Blue Shirts and defeated Preto, who was deported to Spain in 1934. But in September 1935, at about the same time Pessoa penned his satiric anti-Salazar poems, an extreme right-wing group that included a number of former Blue Shirts took up arms against the regime and attempted a coup.[17] Between the time that Preto was deported and the attempted coup, Pessoa wrote an autobiographical sketch in which he noted that *O Interregno* "deve ser considerado como não existente" [should be considered nonexistent] (3:1428). This notation seems to confirm his unhappiness with the dictatorship, but it is far from clear that he was a proponent of liberal democracy or socialism.

In any case, Pessoa never published his anti-Salazar poems, and, with the exception of his critique of a government ban on secret societies, he never openly attacked the dictatorship in any way. Perhaps because he had remained silent, the editing of his work received financial backing from the regime. Notwithstanding Salazar's adulation of Camões, the nation took pride in the "discovery" of Pessoa, whose work was interpreted along nationalistic lines and reprinted in government publications.[18] Pessoa himself would surely have been amazed at the extent to which his work would become associated with Salazar. Indeed, he became such an esteemed poet that in 1969 the government mandated the publication of a definitive inventory of the contents of his trunk.[19]

I have speculated in some detail about Pessoa's politics in the 1930s because after his death he became a symbol of the nation's culture, and his authorship conferred a kind of dignity on the Salazar regime. His nationalistic verse, his indirect homage to Camões in *Mensagem,* and his many poems about traditional life in the Portuguese countryside made him especially attractive to a conservative government. By the 1960s, he had become a monumental figure, more important than a mere politician; he was studied in schools, and he was somehow linked to the identity of the nation itself.

Thus when Salazar passed from the scene, critics were faced with a challenge: either the old Pessoa had to be reduced in stature or a new Pessoa had to be created. The latter course was the one most critics took. With the overthrow of the Salazar-Caetano regime on April 25, 1974, and the installation of a left-wing military government, Pessoa's image took on a new and radically different cast. Following the revolution, a cultural industry formed around the poet, the likes of which was unprecedented in the nation's history.

A few weeks after the revolution, Jorge de Sena, who had been living in self-exile in the United States, published Pessoa's anti-Salazar and Estado Novo poems in *Seara Nova* [New harvest], a journal associated with the opposition during the regime. Given the sentiments of these poems and their dates, Pessoa easily could be presented as one of the earliest critics of the dictatorship. (The poems also made a nice contrast with *O Interregno,* which tended to be ignored after the revolution.) In due course, other previously unpublished materials began appearing in support of an antifascist Pessoa. Not everyone agreed with this interpretation, but even critics like Alfredo Margarido, who considered Pessoa to be right-wing, tended to argue that great poetry transcends politics.[20] This situation was all the more ironic given the fact that Pessoa, like all the other high-modernists, had already been subjected to a traditionally Marxist attack: Mário Sacramento, in *Fernando Pessoa, Poeta da Hora Absurda* (1958), had charged the poet with being an incorrigible aesthete. In the final analysis, however, Pessoa's work was so vast, complex, and contradictory that he easily could be molded to fit any new government.

In 1972 and 1980 respectively, Portugal celebrated the four hundredth anniversary of the publication of *Os Lusíadas* and the death of Camões. Nevertheless, the postrevolutionary government was disinclined to adopt the poet of the empire as its literary symbol. Pessoa, on the other hand, was a modern writer who could represent a new leadership and its hope to transform Portugal. One sign of Pessoa's importance to the government was the establishment of a Center for Pessoa Studies in Oporto shortly after the revolution. The journal of the center, entitled *Persona,* became an important source of postrevolutionary scholarship on the poet, and it initiated the full-scale academic industry that exists today. Among the essays it published were studies of Pessoa's politics and psychology, along with numerous comparative analyses of Pessoa and other major authors, including Camões, Dante, and Whitman. In addition to special sections devoted to translations and previously unpublished materials, it also featured a section dedicated to "polemics" among scholars about the editing and translation of Pessoa's work. *Persona* was generally liberal in tone, allowing many different interpretations to collect around an author who was regarded as canonical.

In the years following the revolution, as Portugal became a full-scale Western democracy, Pessoa began to emerge internationally as a major poet. Among his earliest advocates were the Brazilian modernist Cecília Meireles, who included him in her 1944 anthology of "new" Portuguese poetry; the Prague School theorist Roman Jakobson, who, with Italian critic Luciana Stegnano Picchio, published one of the first important critical studies of Pessoa in French; and the Mexican poet and critic Octavio Paz, who edited and translated an anthology of Pessoa's poems, introducing them with his own seminal essay "El Desconocido de Si Mismo" [To himself unknown]. Recognition of Pessoa in the English-speaking world had begun in the mid-1950s with Edouard Roditi's article (with translations), entitled "The Several Names of Fernando Pessoa," which appeared in the influential Chicago literary magazine *Poetry*. Pessoa's translators in England during the early 1970s included Jonathan Griffin, Peter Rickard, and Roy Campbell; his translators in America were Thomas Merton, Jean Longland, and more importantly, Edwin Honig, who published *Selected Poems by Fernando Pessoa* in 1971.[21] A growing scholarship on Pessoa also emerged in the United States during the 1970s—especially in the form of international conferences dedicated to his works, the first of which was organized in 1977 at Brown University.

In 1985, special events in honor of the fifty years since Pessoa's death were held at the George Pompidou Center in Paris, at the Shaw Theater in London, at the Juan March Foundation in Madrid, and at Vanderbilt University in Nashville, Tennessee. An exhibit at the Pompidou Center featured a "Letter to Fernando Pessoa" from Jorge Luis Borges, who wrote that his Portuguese heritage gave him a sympathetic understanding of the poet from Lisbon (3:1381). In Portugal, there were major exhibits at the Biblioteca Nacional and the Calouste Gulbenkian Foundation, which hosted the Third International Conference on Pessoa. Of all the celebrations that year, however, one in particular took precedence: in recognition of Pessoa's importance as Portugal's major literary figure, President Mário Soares presided over the transference of Pessoa's remains to the Jerónimos, where they were placed near those of Camões.

Between 1985 and 1986, four new editions of Pessoa's "complete" works appeared in Lisbon, along with anthologies, critical studies, and a new edition of Caeiro's O *Guardador de Rebanhos*. But not everyone was happy with the national attention and publication frenzy. By this time, Pessoa had become such an established figure that the younger generation needed to make some kind of iconoclastic gesture, questioning his greatness and establishing their own identity. Among those who made their dissatisfaction known were Mário de Carvalho, who wrote an article entitled "Tanto Pessoa Já Enjoa" [So much Pessoa is nauseating], and Mário Cláudio, organizer of a new edition of António Nobre's *Só*, who proclaimed "Nobre Maior que Pessoa" [Nobre greater than Pessoa].

Despite these occasional attempts to challenge prevailing opinion, Pessoa's reputation grew at an extraordinary rate, until a private, elite, and in some ways rather hermetic poet became a kind of historical hero, equivalent to Washington or Lincoln in the United States. By the late 1980s, Pessoa's face regularly appeared in magazines, newspapers, and on television; it was also put on the one-hundred-escudos note, the Portuguese equivalent of the one-dollar bill. The heteronyms became the subject for paintings and sketches by some of Portugal's premiere artists, and two Pessoa films were released—*Mensagem*, based on the poem, and *Conversa Acabada* [Conversation over], about Pessoa's friendship with Mário de Sá-Carneiro. Like Camões during the Salazar regime, Pessoa was the subject of busts and statues erected throughout the country—among them, a life-size replica of the poet sitting at a table outside the Brasileira Café in the Chiado, Lisbon's oldest and most fashionable shopping district. This particular statue has become a major tourist attraction, enabling people to photograph one another sitting at the table alongside a national monument. More recently, the Casa Pessoa, a sort of museum and shrine, has been founded in the house where Pessoa lived, containing a library, permanent exhibits, and personal objects such as Pessoa's spectacles; and a university now bears his name in Oporto.

Portugal's entry into the European Economic Community in 1986, which brought considerable investment capital to the country, further assisted the growing Pessoa industry. In places such as France and Belgium, which had large Portuguese communities and a number of Portuguese intellectuals who were former exiles, there was immediate interest in Pessoa. In 1986, his complete works were translated into French and published in Paris; and at the Europália–1991 festivities in Brussels, Pessoa was prominently featured in translations, exhibits, catalogs, and special editions. He was an even greater attraction at the EEC celebrations in June 1994, which were hosted by Lisbon as that year's "cultural capital" of Europe. One journalist wrote an article in which he pointed out that Pessoa had been born on the same day as the "*other* Fernando António," Saint Anthony, who is the patron saint of Lisbon.

The widespread interest in Pessoa was evident in many books on the poet, which were widely reviewed and which often became bestsellers. During the period 1985 to 1995, the Lisbon newspaper, *Jornal de Letras, Artes e Ideias*, published more than fifty articles on Pessoa, representing every new critical movement, including deconstruction. (One of the items was illustrated by a facsimile of Roland Barthes's calling card, on which he had penned a note about his fondness for Pessoa.) Especially well publicized in the *Jornal de Letras* and in journals such as *Colóquio* are previously unpublished materials by the poet. Each new "find" is treated as a treasure. Because of the sheer volume of the archive, not to mention the materials in private collections, there seems no end to the Pessoa gold mine.

As happens with most industries where profit and cultural capital are involved (the academic-publishing world notwithstanding), the editing and translation of Pessoa in the last several years has led to fierce struggles among experts. Among the events that added fuel to the often fiery disputes was the creation in 1988 of the "Pessoa Team," or "Equipa Pessoa," which would be responsible for a critical edition of his work.[22] Scholars who were excluded from the team were disappointed and upset; and the fact that members of the editorial committee were officially appointed by Secretary of Culture Teresa Patrícia Gouveia only increased the tension. Few specialists seemed to disagree that a new edition, free as possible of errors and supplemented with new materials, was desirable. The question under debate was who were the individuals best qualified to carry out this task; some writers also asked whether an edition that made any claims at being definitive was even possible, considering the fragmentary and incomplete nature of Pessoa's opus.[23]

In the midst of the various disagreements over these and other issues, the novelist Augusto Abelaira wrote an amusing yet thoughtful commentary entitled "Qual Fernando Pessoa?" [Which Fernando Pessoa?] dealing with the problems faced by the common reader. Abelaira describes himself as so bewildered by the anthologies and editions of Pessoa that line his bookshelves, that he can no longer choose one to read. He also expresses a certain nostalgia for the days of the Ática edition, which, despite its errors, presented "o Pessoa que me deslumbrou" [the Pessoa who overwhelmed me].[24] What Abelaira's critique reveals is the shift in focus from the pleasures of reading and studying Pessoa as a fully constructed author to the more onerous and perplexing task of deciding what authorship means and whether it can be sustained in Pessoa's case.

This problem became especially clear in 1990, when the Equipa Pessoa and Teresa Rita Lopes each published a new edition of Álvaro de Campos, honoring the centenary of his "birth." Lopes wrote an article in *Colóquio*, attacking the Equipa Pessoa edition; and the Equipa (Berardinelli and Castro) responded with a defense of their work, which was published in pamphlet form. The polemic moved to a *Jornal de Letras* interview with Lopes, who accused the Equipa Pessoa of benefiting from her volume on Campos. A response followed by Luiz Fagundes Duarte of the Equipa Pessoa, who claimed that Lopes had benefited from *their* work. Equally contentious was a debate that broke out around the same time between Teresa Sobral Cunha and Richard Zenith about the *Livro do Desassossego*. Cunha had participated in the Ática version, and between 1991 and 1992, she had organized a new, two-volume edition which was published as part of the Presença series entitled "Ler Pessoa" [To read Pessoa]. Her edition was reviewed by Zenith in *Colóquio*. Zenith had prepared an English translation of *Livro*, and he raised several questions and objections concerning Cunha's editorial decisions. Cunha responded in an article in the *Jornal de*

Letras, pointing out that Zenith's translation had benefited from her work, even though he did not give her proper credit. Cunha also lamented the fact that four different English translations of the *Livro* had appeared that year, creating an overcrowded and confused "feira literária" [literary market-place], which would detract from the work itself. Zenith responded with a somewhat glib "letter" to Cunha, pointing out the differences between his translation and her work. The critic Eugénio Lisboa then entered the fray, with a severe commentary to his "friend" Cunha, whom he felt had misrepresented his role as editor of the Carcanet series which had published Zenith's translation. He also argued that there was nothing wrong with the simultaneous appearance of four different English translations, since translation is an art rather than a science.

There can be no question of the importance of Cunha's new edition as a whole: it included previously unpublished material, it reordered texts, and it corrected numerous errors made in the Ática transcription. Having worked with the Pessoa archive for many years, Cunha is considered by many as the foremost authority on Pessoa's handwriting. (It is also fair to state that Zenith's English rendition of the *Livro* is the best of the four translations.) One can find similar quarrels in the history of Shakespeare scholarship, and it seems only natural to expect disputes whenever the text of a major national poet needs to be fixed. Indeed the exchange between Cunha and Zenith was mild compared to the furor that erupted after Európália–1991 in Brussels, where a catalog entitled *L'Univers Pessoa* was prepared by Pierre Léglise-Costa with the participation of eminent scholars such as Eduardo Prado Coelho. This catalog sparked one of the most vituperative arguments to date about the nature of Pessoa's work.

The debate over *L'Univers Pessoa* was initiated by Teresa Rita Lopes, in an essay entitled "Pessoa Normalizado para Uso da CEE" [Pessoa normalized for the use of the EEC], which was published in the *Jornal de Letras.* Lopes wrote a critique of the catalog in the form of an imaginary "conversation" between Pessoa and Álvaro de Campos, who has supposedly just returned to Lisbon from the Európália event. The conversation focuses on Campos's anger at the "cretinos" [cretins] who have provided incorrect information on Pessoa and the heteronyms and misrepresented their works in the catalog.

Lopes's "review" provoked an indignant and highly personalized response from Coelho and Léglise-Costa, who described her as an overbearing, hysterical mother angry at not having been consulted or included in a publication on Pessoa. Lopes's "dialogue" may have in fact grown out of her professional pique; nevertheless, Coelho and Léglise-Costa's rebuttal was needlessly abusive and chauvinistic. Moreover, they failed to address the many inaccuracies that Campos had pointed out in his "conversation" with Pessoa. Lopes responded with a second "conversation," referring to Coelho as "Conselheiro Coelho" [Counselor Coelho] and his coauthor, Léglise-Costa, as a "cu-autor" [asshole author]. The conflict eventually subsided with the publication of an article by the Brazilian Leyla Perrone Moisés, one of the contributors to *L'Univers Pessoa,* who complained that her study of Pessoa had been poorly rendered into French and that even some of her remarks had been changed in the translation process.

What the various quarrels over Pessoa's collected writings were beginning to signify was not simply academic rivalry or the differing claims of editorial "science" (though of course those motives may have been present). The fact is, there were now so many editions and translations that Pessoa was beginning to undergo a kind of indirect deconstruction. His work, which was once so solid, was beginning to turn back into a "text"— a vast discursive activity that no metalanguage could control and that the author, in the words of Barthes, could only "visit" as a "guest."[25]

Despite this phenomenon, new editions of Pessoa's work have continued to appear, and debates surrounding their organization and accuracy continue to be waged. He is now a major international poet, and his very instability or multiplicity makes him increasingly appropriate to a postmodern world. In the future, every new development in literary theory will generate new readings of the texts that he wrote. On the Internet, there are already discussions among specialists outside Portugal about the place of Pessoa in queer studies. Just as the right and left in Portugal constructed a national poet to fit their respective political agendas, there is every reason to believe that gender studies will construct a convincing "queer" Pessoa to contrast with the "straight" Pessoa of the love letters to Ophélia. Perhaps one day, the internecine struggles over Pessoa in journals and supplements will give way to a cyberspace battle on the Internet—a "virtual" contest over the "real" nature of a poet who would have been amused and delighted to see how many new faces he could acquire.

All this is not to suggest that Pessoa can be made to signify anything his critics desire. On the contrary, it is quite possible and even worthwhile to reconstruct Pessoa's general aims and aesthetic attitudes from the considerable body of essays, correspondence, and criticism he left behind. The poetry of his major heteronyms can be arranged into relatively unified volumes, which are subject to the same kind of analysis we give to any other writer. Moreover, it seems to me important to speculate about Pessoa's politics and sexuality, because such matters have an important bearing on how we understand the verse. When I refer to the possible creation of a "queer Pessoa," I do not want to trivialize the work of critics or to diminish what could be a significant new line of interpretation. My point is simply that all literature is polyvalent, filled with contradictions and tensions that enable it to survive in the discursive economy, and with meanings that emerge as social conditions change. The "great authors" are complex figures, situated in contradictory historical moments, open to a variety of uses. The critics who construct Pessoa and interpret his works are therefore not manufacturing his personality out of thin air. The meanings and structures they produce are in some sense "there," like historical traces. But which of these multifarious traces—which "faces" of Pessoa—shall we emphasize at any given time? The answer seems to me to depend upon our own history or on the issues that are important to us at our moment. The critical/biographical/editorial enterprise is by no means chimerical; but we should recognize that it is a social activity, subject to historical determinants—an activity that tells us as much about ourselves as about the remarkable artists we study.

Notes

Introduction

1. For an earlier discussion of the relationship between the major heteronyms, see Coelho, *Diversidade*. Another discussion, somewhat closer to my own view, can be found in Seabra, *Fernando Pessoa*.

2. The books were: *35 Sonnets* (1918), *Antinous* (1918), and two volumes entitled *English Poems I–II* (1921) and *English Poems III. Epithalamium* (1921). In September 1918, the *London Times* and the *Glasgow Herald* favorably reviewed Pessoa's *35 Sonnets,* which the *Times* commended for its "Ultra-Shakespearean Shakespeareanisms" and "Tudor tricks of repetition, involution, and antithesis" (quoted in Rickard, "Fernando Pessoa," 44). Two years later, his poem "Meantime" was published in *The Athenaeum*.

3. Unless otherwise indicated, quotations from Pessoa's writings, cited parenthetically in the text, are from the three-volume *Obra Poética e em Prosa,* ed. Quadros and Pereira da Costa. In the transcription of citations in Portuguese, outdated orthographies have been replaced with contemporary versions.

4. Pessoa, *Cartas a Cortes-Rodrigues,* 46.

5. Teresa Sobral Cunha followed a similar design in her 1994 edition of Caeiro (*Poemas Completos de Alberto Caeiro*).

6. Foucault, "What Is an Author?" 147, 151.

7. Barthes, "Death of the Author," 143.

Chapter 1: Pessoa's Juvenilia and the Origins of "Heteronymous" Poetry

1. For a concise overview of the juvenilia, see Silveira, "Fernando Pessoa."

2. The literature on this subject is extensive. Among the more important commentators are Roland Barthes, who argues that every text is filled with anonymous citations from items that are already read. Harold Bloom emphasizes the conscious, willful use of antecedent materials by writers who are contending with strong influences. Along similar lines, Tzvetan Todorov has claimed that genre conventions are remade by literary artists, and Umberto Eco argues that the reader's intertextual knowledge can be used by certain writers who "over code" their work. For an interesting discussion of how intertextuality establishes hierarchies and canons, see Collins, *Uncommon Cultures,* especially 46–49.

3. A facsimile of the newspaper version can be found in *Fotobibliografia,* 25. There are a few minor differences between the poem published in *O Imparcial* and the version that appears in Pessoa's *Obra Poética,* 1:145–46.

4. In her study of the *Cancioneiro Geral,* Andrée Crabbé Rocha observes that "poesia obrigada a mote" constituted a "mode of intertextuality" that functioned as a sign of the poet's literary competence or "index of culture" (27, 29). Court poets demonstrated the breadth of their poetic memory by means of the quotation in the *mote,* as well as by the ideas, images, and expressions appropriated from other sources and woven into the *glosa.* The audience was also invited to acquire cultural capital, since the "mote e glosa" challenged listeners (in this case, the nobility) to identify the source of the *mote* and to detect traces of other sources in the *glosa.*

5. An examination of the *Cancioneiro Geral* reveals that the source of the *mote* usually was not indicated. This was because the poet either wanted to challenge the audience or no longer remembered the source. Pessoa followed this practice, but his audience was not quite up to the challenge. *O Imparcial* incorrectly identified the source of his *mote* as Augusto Vicente. Recently, the critic Pedro da Silveira pointed out that the newspaper should have attributed the opening lines to Augusto Gil (Silveira, "Fernando Pessoa," 98). A widely read poet in his day, Gil wrote both serious and light verse, including "Cartas a Desoras" [Late-night letter], which concerns a lady's distracting décolletage (Gil, *Versos*). One of Gil's best-known works, entitled *O Canto da Cigarra* [Song of the cicada] (1910), is a satire on women that makes ample use of the *glosa.*

6. Numerous examples can be found in the section dedicated to *redondilhas* in Camões, *Obras,* 1:1–186.

7. Pessoa referred to the art of forgery in several contexts, most notably in a fragmentary comment on acting: "We all love a forger. It is a very human and a quite instinctive sentiment" (3:119–20). His use of the term merits comparison with the famous ending of Joyce's *A Portrait of the Artist as a Young Man* (1914), where Stephen Dedalus declares his intention to "forge in the smithy of my soul the uncreated conscience of my race" (253). Pessoa and Joyce seem to be playing upon a double meaning of the word, suggesting both creation and duplication, both originality and imitation.

8. Rickard, "Fernando Pessoa," 47.

9. According to a recent study, Pessoa created at least seventy-two fictional authors. (See Lopes, *Pessoa por Conhecer,* 1:167–69.) But here we might ask, what is an author? As this chapter will demonstrate, Pessoa was in the habit of inventing fictional personalities and pseudonyms from a very early age. There are probably more than one hundred names of such figures in his work, although only four created a large enough body of significant poetry to be considered authors in the normative sense.

10. Numerous books of criticism and exegesis exist on the heteronyms. Among the most widely cited studies in Portuguese are those by Cleonice Berardinelli,

Jacinto do Prado Coelho, Georg Rudolf Lind, Eduardo Lourenço, Adolfo Casais Monteiro, António Quadros, José Augusto Seabra, and Jorge de Sena. George Monteiro and Bernard McGuirk's collections contain essays and bibliographic information on the heteronyms in English.

11. Pessoa saw in the works of Cesário Verde an example of this constructive practice:

> There is a great Portuguese poet called Cesário Verde; he lived in the middle years of the nineteenth century. The whole attitude to life which makes him a great poet can actually be found in anticipation in two casual poems of Guilherme Braga, a poet ten years older than he. But what in Cesário is gathered together into a whole concept of the universe, was a mere chance in Braga's production. And, even if, as is quite probable, Braga's casual poems made Cesário find himself, even if by a plagiarism without plagiarism, the earlier man is nevertheless smaller. (It is the later man who is the earlier.) (3:42–43)

12. Facsimiles of these newspapers appear in Lopes, *Pessoa por Conhecer,* vol. 2.

13. Kristeva, *Desire in Language,* 66.

14. The polemic began in July 1904 with an "imitation" by J. J. Hillier (a former Durban high-school student) of a Horatian ode—a poem that appeared in a column entitled "The Man in the Moon," which was devoted to light verse. Dr. C. H. Haggar, Pessoa's teacher at the Commercial School in Durban, wrote a parody of Hillier's imitation and titled it "The True Story of Horace." Haggar's poem provoked a contribution to "The Man in the Moon" by an author who was identified simply as "Fairplay." Pessoa entered the duel of words and wits with a brief critical appraisal of the poems by Hillier, Haggar, and Fairplay and a parody in verse of all three poets, which he signed "C. R. Anon" (*Fotobibliografia,* 26; Jennings, *Os Dois Exílios,* 48–52).

15. This particular aspect of the newspapers is one of the more obvious manifestations of Pessoa's love of artistic "forgery." Several holograph papers in the Pessoa archive in the Biblioteca Nacional provide further documentation of his fascination with signatures: names and abbreviated versions of names for his various heteronyms appear written, crossed out, and rewritten in the margins of papers, and they often cover entire pages. Forever playing with and perfecting the names and signatures of his heteronyms, he was also intent on giving them special handwritings—a technique that seems to date back to *A Palavra* and *O Palrador.* The archive also contains several fragments in English on handwriting, one of which is entitled "Essay on Character in Handwriting."

16. The fictional names invented by Pessoa are often playful anagrams. Fr. (Friar) Angard might be a variation on Angra, the capital of Terceira, where Pessoa stayed with relatives, but it is more likely a phonetic respelling of the French "en garde." Dr. Calviro is probably a play on "Calvino," or Calvin.

17. Pessoa's inclination toward using amusing names for many of his authors is

most likely derived from Dickens and more specifically from the *Pickwick Papers*.

18. Lopes, *Pessoa por Conhecer*, 2:130–31.

19. For additional commentary on Poe and Pessoa, consult George Monteiro, "Poe/Pessoa."

20. Nobre, *Só*, 170.

21. Sena, *Fernando Pessoa*, 83.

22. Lopes, *Pessoa por Conhecer*, 2:134, 136.

23. Kristeva, *Desire in Language*, 69.

Chapter 2: Nationalism, Modernism, and the Formation of Pessoa's Aesthetic

1. Cunha, "Pessoa: Diário," 80.

2. Family members often called him "Ibis"—a nickname he acquired because of his playful imitation of the tall, thin, storklike bird that stands on one foot.

3. A diary fragment with the heading "Plan of Life" reveals Pessoa's meager circumstances and his preoccupation with the yearly budget:

> A general plan of life must involve, in the first place, the obtaining of a financial stability of some kind. I put the limit needed for the humble thing I call financial stability at about sixty dollars, forty being for the necessary, and twenty for the superfluous things of life. The way to obtain this is to add to the thirty-one dollars from the two offices (P & FF) twenty-nine other dollars, the origin of which is to be determined. Rigorously, to just live, fifty dollars would do, for, taking thirty-five as a necessary basis, fifteen would cover the rest. (2:88)

4. Perloff, *The Futurist Moment*, xix.

5. For a comprehensive study of this period in Portuguese history, see Wheeler, *Republican Portugal*.

6. Several well-known intellectuals participated in this revolt, including the philosopher Sampaio Bruno and the republican writer, Basílio Teles—who, according to historian Manuel Villaverde Cabral, were two of the most prominent nationalist ideologues in late-nineteenth- and early-twentieth-century Portugal (see Cabral, "Aesthetics of Nationalism," 17.)

7. Gallagher, *Portugal*, 18.

8. Quoted in Wheeler, *Republican Portugal*, 62.

9. King Sebastião ruled Portugal from 1554 to 1578. A young and impetuous ruler, he led a crusade against the much larger Islamic forces in Morocco and was resoundingly defeated. Struck down in battle, his body was never found. Sebastião had no heirs, leaving the door open to King Felipe of Spain, who claimed his right to the throne and forcibly annexed Portugal in 1580. For the next sixty years, the country was under Spanish rule. Sebastião's demise and the loss of independence marked the end of Portugal's "Golden Age." The unhappiness of the Portuguese (especially the poor and working class) during the period of Spanish control fostered the myth that Sebastião was still alive and would return to save his people. For

further information on Sebastianism, see Antunes, *Saudade e Profetismo;* Brooks, *A King for Portugal;* Serrão, *Do Sebastianismo;* Sousa, "Pessoa the Messenger"; and Suárez, "Portugal's *Saudosismo* Movement."

10. Wheeler, *Republican Portugal,* 17; 278, n. 23. Wheeler notes that the close association between republicanism and Sebastianism, or what became known as "republican Sebastianism" (especially in the year preceding the republic), could be detected in the language of republican leaders like Teófilo Braga, which tended to be messianic. Wheeler also mentions that the lower classes in Lisbon believed that messianic pamphlets circulating before the republic foretold its imminent arrival.

11. In a diary fragment dated 1908, two years prior to the revolution, Pessoa wrote of his profound but frustrated sense of personal mission to improve his country's situation: "My intense patriotic suffering, my intense desire of bettering the condition of Portugal provoke in me—how to express with what warmth, with what intensity, with what sincerity!—a thousand plans which, even if one man could realise them, he had to have one characteristic which in me is purely negative—the power of will" (2:78). The diary reveals that his "plans" were formidable. Among other things, he hoped to incite a revolt: "Beside my patriotic projects—writing of 'Portugal Republic'—to provoke a revolution here, writing of Portuguese pamphlets, editing of older national literary works, creation of a magazine, of a scientific review, etc.—other plans, consuming me with the necessity of being soon carried out . . . combine to produce an excess of impulse that paralyses my will. The suffering that this produces I know not if it can be described as on this side of insanity" (2:79).

Both entries in the diary convey a frenzied ambition and passionate, almost Hamletesque paralysis of "will" that Pessoa describes as if it were akin to madness. (Throughout his life, his correspondence frequently alludes to his fear of losing his reason—a fear that can be traced back to his memories of his maternal grandmother, who suffered from severe mental illness.) He was probably also comparing himself to the popular image of Portugal's lost king, Sebastião, whose national fervor and visions of greatness were often depicted as a sort of *afflatus,* or inspired insanity. Years later, in one of the most widely cited poems in the sequence published as *Mensagem,* Pessoa would celebrate this mania, which supposedly caused Sebastião to lead his troops into an unwinnable battle.

12. In his essay entitled "O Espírito Lusitano ou o Saudosismo" [The Lusitanian spirit or saudosismo], Pascoaes said he preferred the definition provided by the late-fifteenth-century chronicler, Duarte Nunes de Leão, in his *Origem da Língua Portuguesa* [Origin of the Portuguese language] ("Saudade é lembrança de alguma coisa com desejo dela" [Saudade is the memory of something with the desire for it]) over the "more restricted" definition given by romantic poet Almeida Garrett ("gosto amargo" [bitter pleasure] or "dor e alegria" [pain and happiness]); see Pascoaes, *A Saudade e o Saudosismo,* 50. In his poetry, Pessoa tended to move back and forth between both definitions. For instance, in one poem he writes: "Eu amo tudo o que foi, / Tudo o que já não é . . . " [I love everything that was, / Everything

that no longer is . . .] (1:328); while in another, he states: "Não é alegria nem dor esta dor com que me alegro" [It's neither happiness nor pain this pain that makes me happy] (1:166).

13. According to historian and critic Joel Serrão, the Portuguese philosopher Sampaio Bruno's book about Sebastianism, entitled *O Encoberto* (1904) [The hidden one], was extremely influential in the formulation of *saudosismo;* see Coelho, *Dicionário,* 1006.

14. Pascoaes, *A Saudade e o Saudosismo,* 36–37.

15. Ibid., 44. For more on this subject, see Antunes, *Saudade e Profetismo.*

16. On *Orpheu,* see Crespo, *A Vida Plural,* 86. Lind, *Estudos sobre Pessoa,* 19.

17. Pascoaes, *A Saudade e o Saudosismo,* 37. There are other points of contact between the *saudosistas* and the *integralistas;* particularly interesting are the mysticism and messianism that pervade their respective writings.

18. Júdice, *Era,* 25.

19. A facsimile of the poem as it appeared in *A Renascença* can be found in *Fotobibliografia,* 41.

20. The term *neogarrettismo,* coined by the poet Alberto de Oliveira in 1892, was frequently used to identify the latent romanticism of late-nineteenth- and early-twentieth-century writers like the *saudosistas,* who wished to abandon foreign models and return to traditional sources (see Coelho, *Dicionário,* 711). The critic Maria Aliete Galhoz also cites Poe's "The Bells" and the nineteenth-century Portuguese poet Luís Augusto Palmeirim's "Recordação da Infância" [Memories of childhood] as other possible sources of inspiration for this poem (Galhoz, "Em Torno ao Poema de Pessoa," 743–57).

21. Simões, *Vida e Obra de Pessoa,* 191; Júdice, *Era,* 34.

22. Sa-Carneiro, *Cartas,* vol. 1, 116.

23. Pessoa published "Chuva Oblíqua" under his own name in *Orpheu* in 1915; twenty years later, in his letter on the heteronyms, he affirmed that Pessoa "himself" was the author (2:341). However, in October 1914, just months after the official appearance of the heteronyms, he wrote his friend Armando Cortes-Rodrigues that "Chuva Oblíqua" was by Álvaro de Campos (Pessoa, *Cartas a Cortes-Rodrigues,* 170).

24. For a useful (though controversial) discussion of the dialectical process in modern art history as a whole, see Bürger, *Theory of the Avant-Garde,* especially 78–82. In Bürger's terms, the aesthetic I am describing remains fully within the conventional notions of the "organic" work of art. As Bürger puts it, this sort of art is always constructed so that "individual parts and the whole form a dialectical unity." In some respects, Pessoa's writing could also be seen from a more avant-garde perspective, so that the parts do not cohere and true unity is never achieved. I have tried to suggest this potential tendency of his work by indicating that the poem under discussion is somewhat like a montage.

25. In an introduction to Pessoa's writings on the republic, Joel Serrão remarks that Pessoa's vision of Portugal's cultural renewal was influenced by Hegel ("Da República Portuguesa e de Pessoa nela," 59, n. 2).

26. Pessoa described the scandal that *Orpheu* had created in a letter to Cortes-Rodrigues, who had contributed to *Orpheu* from the Azores:

> *Foi um triunfo absoluto,* especialmente com o reclame que *A Capital* nos fez com uma tareia na primeira página, um artigo de duas colunas . . . Naturalmente temos que fazer segunda edição. *"Somos o assunto do dia em Lisboa"*; sem exagero lho digo. O escândalo é enorme. Somos apontados na rua, e toda a gente—mesmo extra-literária—fala no *Orpheu* . . .
>
> O escândalo maior tem sido causado pelo *16* de Sá-Carneiro e a *Ode Triunfal* . . . (Pessoa, *Cartas a Cortes-Rodrigues,* 63, 65)

[It was an absolute triumph, especially with the protest that *The Capital* (a daily newspaper in Lisbon) made against us in a front page attack that was two columns long . . . Naturally we have to do a second edition. *"We're the talk of all Lisbon"*; I say this to you without exaggeration. The scandal is enormous. We're pointed out on the street, and everybody—even non-literary types—are talking about *Orpheu* . . .

The biggest scandal has been caused by Sá-Carneiro's *16* and by the *Triumphal Ode.]*

27. Júdice, "Futurismo," viii.

28. The second issue of *Orpheu* is filled with deliberately controversial items by such figures as Ângelo de Lima, who was confined to an insane asylum; Raul Leal, who had scandalized Lisbon by publicly declaring his homosexuality; and "um anónimo ou anónima que diz chamar-se Violante Cysneiros" [an anonymous man or woman who goes by the name Violante Cysneiros], who was actually Pessoa's close friend Cortes-Rodrigues. Besides this poetry and prose, there were also photographs of artwork by the futurist-inspired Santa Rita Pintor.

Interseccionismo was defined early on by Pessoa as a more serious form of *paúlismo,* and it was officially announced with the publication of "Chuva Oblíqua" in *Orpheu.* According to Lind, *interseccionismo* was in the mold of other avant-garde tendencies of the period 1910–1912, such as syncronism (Marcello Fabri and Nicolas Bauduin) and simultaneanism (Martin Barzun). It also had certain affinities with Rimbaud's "técnica da intercalação" [technique of intercalation]. The latter involves the "intersection" of two normally heterogeneous entities—as in Rimbaud's poem "Marine," where the images of land and sea become indistinguishable. (For a discussion of *interseccionismo* and *paúlismo,* see Lind, *Estudos sobre Pessoa,* 39–77.)

Within a year, Pessoa had abandoned *interseccionismo* for what he described as *sensacionismo.* Ultimately, it is less important to detail the programs of these various "isms" than to recognize that the period in question was marked by the tendency of poets througout Europe to form short-lived movements. For example, in 1912 F. S. Flint wrote a lengthy essay for the British journal *The Poetry Review,* in which he provided an encyclopedic review of new French "schools," including *Neo-Mallarmisme, Futurisme, L'Impulsionisme, Les Paroxystes, Les Fantasistes,* etc. Shortly after this article, the Anglo-American poets in Flint's circle announced the formation of their own movement, called "imagism."

29. Campos later satirized Marinetti's nomination to the Italian Academy of Letters in an undated poem entitled "Marinetti, Académico" [Marinetti, academician]:

> Lá chegam todos, lá chegam todos . . .
> Qualquer dia, salvo venda, chego eu também . . .
> Se nascem, afinal, todos para isso . . .
>
> Não tenho remédio senão morrer antes,
> Não tenho remédio senão escalar o Grande Muro . . .
> Se fico cá, prendem-me para ser social . . .
>
> Lá chegam todos, porque nasceram para Isso,
> E só se chega ao Isso para que se nasceu . . .
>
> Lá chegam todos . . .
> Marinetti, académico . . .
>
> As Musas vingaram-se com focos eléctricos, meu velho,
> Puseram-te por fim na ribalta da cave velha,
> E a tua dinâmica, sempre um bocado italiana, f-f-f-f-f-f-f-f . . . (1:1038)
>
> [There everyone arrives, there everyone arrives . . .
> Any day, safely blindfolded, I too will arrive . . .
> In the final analysis, everyone is born for that . . .
>
> I have no choice but to die beforehand,
> I have no choice but to scale the Great Wall . . .
> If I stay here, they'll apprehend me in order to be social . . .
>
> There everyone arrives, because everyone was born for That,
> And one only arrives at That for which one is born . . .
>
> There everyone arrives . . .
> Marinetti, academician . . .
>
> The Muses avenged themselves with electric foci, old fellow,
> They finally put you at the footlights of the old cave,
> And your dynamic, always slightly Italian, f-f-f-f-f-f-f-f . . .]

30. Among the papers in Pessoa's archive is a three-page typed letter in English to Marinetti, which was incorrectly attributed to Pessoa in an early edition of his work, and again more recently by Edwin Honig in the anthology *Fernando Pessoa Always Astonished*. The letter was actually composed by Raul Leal, who wrote to Marinetti about futurism's unwise proposition to jettison the past. The fact that Pessoa translated Leal's lengthy letter into English might be interpreted as a sign of

Pessoa's agreement with Leal's point of view.

31. A third issue was ready to be printed in 1916, but the loss of financial backing that occurred with Sá-Carneiro's death prevented it from appearing.

32. *Portugal Futurista*, 30, 32.

33. Gallagher, *Portugal*, 25.

34. Pascoaes, *A Saudade e o Saudosismo*, 107.

35. See Cabral, "Aesthetics of Nationalism," for a general assessment of Pessoa's politics.

Chapter 3: The Poetry of Fernando Pessoa

1. In a letter written to Cortes-Rodrigues on September 2, 1914, Pessoa was already speaking of the heteronyms as if they were all old friends (*Cartas a Cortes-Rodrigues*, 34).

2. In an interview published in 1926, Pessoa remarked that Portugal's cultural tradition was limited to the period from the Middle Ages to the early Renaissance, when the *Cancioneiros* and novels of chivalry were produced (3:708).

3. I have omitted discussion of these verses, choosing to emphasize Pessoa's fascination with the occult and mysterious in my remarks on *Mensagem*. A detailed treatment of the esoteric verses may be found in Costa, *O Esoterismo*.

4. Pascoaes, *A Saudade e o Saudosismo*, 80.

5. Impressed with the high quality of *Mensagem*, the jury increased the prize from one thousand to five thousand escudos—the equivalent of the award for best long submission, which went to the Franciscan priest, Vasco Reis, for a long anti-Communist work entitled *Romaria* (Pilgrimage). In January 1935, Pessoa published a review of this poem, declaring it "adorável" [adorable] (3:1281–3). For further critical commentary on *Mensagem* see, for example, Almeida, *Mensagem*, as well as the bibliography by Blanco in Pessoa, *Mensagem—Poemas Esotéricos*.

6. In the same interview, Pessoa was asked to comment on the periods of great literary creativity in Portugal. His response is symptomatic: "O Infante, Albuquerque e os outros semideuses da nossa glória esperam ainda o seu cantor" [The Infante, Albuquerque and the other demigods of our glorious past still await their singer]—a declaration that he followed up with the following pronouncement: "Há só um período de criação na nossa história literária: não chegou ainda" [There's only one period of creation in our literary history: it still hasn't arrived] (see 3:702–3).

7. Modernist writers as different as Joyce and Brecht have agreed that epic poetry is defined by its narration; thus Joyce's Stephen Dedalus describes the classical epic as a type of verse in which "the personality of the artist passes into the narration itself, flowing round and round the persons and the actions like a vital sea."

8. In the fragment, "O Império Espiritual" [The spiritual empire], which appears alongside two other items for his projected "Manifesto sobre o Atlantismo" [Manifesto on Atlanticism], Pessoa wrote: "Criando uma civilização espiritual própria, subjugaremos todos os povos; porque contra as artes e as forças do espírito não há

resistência possível, sobretudo quando elas sejam bem organizadas, fortificadas por almas de generais do Espírito" [By creating our own spiritual civilization, we will subjugate all peoples; because there is no possible resistance against the arts and the forces of the spirit, especially when they are well organized and fortified by souls of generals of the Spirit] (3:682). For further discussion of Pessoa's *Atlantismo,* see 3:681–83 and Santos, "Atlantic Poets."

9. In an interview published in 1926, Pessoa spoke at length about the importance of myth to raising a nation's sense of patriotism. I am quoting a lengthy section of this interview because of its significance to *Mensagem:*

> Há só uma espécie de propaganda com que se pode levantar o moral de uma nação—a construção ou renovação e a difusão consequente e multímoda de um grande mito nacional. De instinto, a humanidade odeia a verdade, porque sabe, com o mesmo instinto, que não há verdade, ou que a verdade é inatingível. O mundo conduz-se por mentiras; quem quiser despertá-lo ou conduzi-lo terá que mentir-lhe delirantemente, e fá-lo-á com tanto mais êxito quanto mais mentir a si mesmo e se compenetrar da verdade da mentira que criou. Temos, felizmente, o mito sebastianista com raízes profundas no passado e na alma portuguesa. Nosso trabalho é pois mais fácil; não temos que criar um mito, senão que renová-lo. Comecemos por nos embebedar desse sonho, por o integrar em nós, por o incarnar. Feito isso, cada um de nós independentemente e a sós consigo, o sonho se derramará sem esforço em tudo que dissermos ou escrevermos, e a atmosfera estará criada, em que todos os outros, como nós, o respirem. Então se dará na alma da Nação o fenómeno imprevisível de onde nascerão as Novas Descobertas, a Criação do Mundo Novo, o Quinto Império. Terá regressado El-Rei D. Sebastião. (3:710)

> [There's only one kind of propaganda with which one can lift a nation's morale—the construction or renovation and consequent, multimode diffusion of a great national myth. By instinct, humanity hates the truth because it knows, with the same instinct, that there is no truth, or that the truth is unattainable. The world is guided by lies; whoever wishes to awaken it or lead it will have to lie deliriously and will do it more successfully the more he lies to himself and is convinced of the truth of the lie that he created. Luckily, we have the Sebastianist myth with deep roots in the past and in the Portuguese soul. Our work is then easier; we do not have to create a myth but to renovate it. Let us begin by intoxicating ourselves with this dream, integrating it into ourselves in order to incarnate it. This done, each one of us independently and by ourselves alone, the dream will effortlessly extend into everything that we say or write, and the atmosphere will be created in which all the others like us, will breathe it. Then the unforeseen phenomenon will take place in the Nation's soul from which will be born the New Discoveries,

the Creation of the New World, the Fifth Empire. King Sebastião will have returned.]

10. The coupling of male and female figures in this section might be related to Pessoa's vision of the "Spiritual Empire," which he portrayed as: "andrógino, reunidor das qualidades masculinas e femininas: imperialismo que seja cheio de todas as subtilezas do domínio feminino e de todas as forças e estruturações do domínio masculino. Realizemos Apolo espiritualmente" [androgynous, assembler of masculine and feminine qualities: imperialism that may be filled with all the subtleties of the female domain and all the forces and structurings of the male domain. Let us realize Apollo spiritually] (3:682).

11. Macedo, "A *Mensagem*," 28.

12. Pessoa wrote extensively on Sebastianism and the Fifth Empire—writings which he intended to include in a book about the prophesies of Bandarra (see 3:611–76). In the section on Dom Sebastião, he recounts a situation similar to the one in the poem "Nevoeiro": "A manhã de nevoeiro. Por manhã entende-se o princípio de qualquer coisa nova—época, fase ou coisa semelhante. Por nevoeiro entende-se que o Desejado virá "encoberto"; que, chegando, se não perceberá que chegou" [Morning of mist. By morning understand the beginning of something new—epoch, phase or a similar thing. By mist understand that the Desired One will come "concealed"; that, arriving, no one will perceive that he has arrived] (3:654).

Pessoa describes the "first coming" as having occurred in 1640, the year in which the Portuguese regained control of their country from Spanish rule, which began the period known as the "Restauração" [Restoration]. He states that the second coming happened in 1888, which ushered in the "Reino do Sol" [Reign of the Sun]. Critics have suggested that, rather than alluding to his own year of birth, Pessoa might have been referring to the founding of the Cabalistic Order of the Rosa-Cruz, which occurred that year. However, given Pessoa's lifelong fascination with prophesy and greatness (not to mention horoscopes), it seems more likely that he selected 1888 as a way of indirectly announcing himself as the country's unrecognized savior.

13. Pessoa, *Quadras*, 7.

14. This poem appears at the end of a letter that Pessoa wrote in English to his friend Armando Teixeira Rebelo. In the text of the letter, Pessoa also made clear his feelings about Portuguese country life: "I sincerely believe that, if I were to remain here for a month, I would have to go to Lisbon, afterwards to [the] Bombarda Hotel. You can hardly imagine the hyperboredom, the ultra-get-tired of-everythingness, the absolute what-the-blooming hell-is-a-chap-to-do-hereability that reigns in my spirit! I found a book to read, but was unable to muster energy to read it. I am anxious to get back to Lisbon; yet I think I will have to stay here yet three days more" (2:128).

15. Pessoa, *Quadras*, 19.

16. In her study of the *Cancioneiro Popular*, Maria Arminda Zaluar Nunes discusses the influence of troubadour love poetry on the development of the folk *quadra* (85–94).

17. Rickard, "Fernando Pessoa"; McGuirk, *Three Persons on One*. See also, for example, Marques, "Fingimento em Cadeia"; George Monteiro, "Song of the Reaper"; Santos, "Poetas e Pássaros"; and Sena, *Fernando Pessoa*.

18. In his preface to *Missal de Trovas*, Pessoa praised the *quadra* as a form derived from what was "instinctivo e desatado da alma popular" [instinctive and free in the popular soul], and as "o vaso de flores que o Povo põe à janela da sua Alma" [the vase of flowers that the People place at the window of their Souls]. The relationship between the *quadra* and Pessoa's popular nationalism is especially apparent in his appraisal of *Missal de Trovas*, whose authors, in his view, "realizaram as suas quadras com destreza lusitana" [realized their *quadras* with Lusitanian dexterity] (see *Fotobibliografia*, 44).

According to Teófilo Braga, whose *História da Poesia Popular Portuguesa* (1867) [History of Portuguese popular poetry] was the first scholarly book on the subject, proverbs were an important source of inspiration for the *quadra;* and in the study *Um Esquema do Cancioneiro Popular Português* (1947) [An outline of the Portuguese popular cancioneiro], the critic Afonso Duarte listed eighty proverbs that were fundamental to the development of the form.

19. Nunes, *O Cancioneiro Popular*, 53.

20. This romantic view of agrarian society appeared in Portuguese literature throughout the nineteenth century and well into the twentieth, and it was a prominent motif in some of Portugal's most revered poets. For example, in Guerra Junqueiro's poem, "Eiras ao Luar" [Threshing floors by moonlight] (*Os Simples* [The simple ones], 1886), reapers are portrayed as "pretty sorceresses" who "dance over the golden wheat." António Nobre's "Canção da Felicidade" [Song of happiness] (*Só*, 1892) sings the praises of peasant life. (The poem's subtitle, "Ideal dum Parisense" [Ideal of a Parisian], is subtly ironic; like many Portuguese intellectuals, Nobre left Portugal for Paris—where he wrote the poem—preferring the modern capital to his preindustrial homeland.) The poet Augusto Gil also wrote poems on this subject: his "Amor Sadio" [Wholesome love] is a about a pretty, healthy, and pregnant peasant to whom the poet pledges his love. Appearing in the volume *Versos*, Gil's poem is accompanied by a fascinating drawing that depicts the extremes of this literary motif. The illustration shows a reaper with a scythe over her shoulder and a bonnet on her head; however, from the neck down she has the look of a Greek goddess, with her breasts bared and her lower body loosely draped with a transparent veil. Interestingly, the figure represented in Gil's book is even more idealized than the stereotypical happy laborer. Instead of joyfully harvesting the wheat, she is descending from on high as if she were the spirit of the field.

21. Pascoaes, *A Saudade e o Saudosismo*, 67.

22. Pessoa might be alluding here to the poet Cesário Verde, whose portraits of the lower class, unlike those of his romantic contemporaries, were far from ideal-

ized. Perhaps this is what the poet and critic Helder Macedo is implying when he mentions in passing Verde's importance to the "Ceifeira" (*Inquérito*, 134).

23. Rickard, "Fernando Pessoa," 47–48.

24. Quoted in Lind, *Estudos sobre Pessoa*, 312–13.

25. Pascoaes, *A Saudade e o Saudosismo*, 91.

Chapter 4: The Poetry of Alberto Caeiro

1. Bloom's thesis, which appears in the chapter "Borges, Neruda, and Pessoa: Hispanic-Portuguese Whitman" in *The Western Canon,* is derived from an unpublished dissertation by Susan Margaret Brown. Unfortunately, Bloom does not credit Brown in his chapter on Pessoa; nor does he seem to know much about the poet beyond what he glibly expounds upon from Brown's work. Unlike Bloom, Brown acknowledges the critic Eduardo Lourenço, who was the first to discuss at length certain affinities between Whitman and Caeiro. From Lourenço's perspective, "Caeiro é um Whitman imaginário, ou antes, um *Whitman em ideia*" [Caeiro is an imaginary Whitman, or rather, a *Whitman without flesh*] (Lourenço, *Pessoa Revisitado,* 44; see Brown, "Poetics of Pessoa's 'Drama em Gente'," 168).

2. Eliot, "Tradition and the Individual Talent," 25, 22.

3. In this chapter, all parenthetical citations that refer to Caeiro are from Teresa Sobral Cunha's excellent critical edition, *Poemas Completos de Alberto Caeiro,* which documents the wide range of materials that Pessoa had prepared to introduce his pagan poet. These include a preface by "the English translator, Thomas Crosse"; prefaces and essays by Ricardo Reis, who was designated as Caeiro's "official editor"; "notes" by Álvaro de Campos; and philosophic essays by António Mora. Among these fascinating materials is a short editorial note, signed by two members of Caeiro's "family," which was to appear at the beginning of his posthumously published complete works. The family members—identified only by the initials "A. L. C." and "J. C."—explain that the book's publication was delayed because Reis had to return to Portugal from America, where he was "um distinto professor de humanidades num importante colégio americano" [a distinguished humanities teacher at an important American school] (21).

Other important documents include two prefaces signed by Reis. One is brief, providing biographical information about the poet and a short commentary on the "reconstructed paganism" that Caeiro's poetry represents. This version ends with a dedication in fulfillment of Caeiro's wishes "à memória de Cesário Verde" [to the memory of Césario Verde] (26), whose work Pessoa praised elsewhere for its incipient *objectivismo.* The longer and more-fragmented preface goes into greater detail about Caeiro's work, commenting on his preference for free verse and how the "rhythmic individuality" of his poems differs from other free-verse poets such as Blake, Whitman, and even Álvaro de Campos. Reis praises Caeiro for the "internal structure" of his poems, stating that he represents what no one ever was—"an absolute objectivist," who "inventou os processos poéticos de todos os tempos . . . os processos filosóficos da nossa época . . . [q]uebrou com todos os sentimentos que têm sido posse da poesia e do pensamento humano" [invented the poetic processes of all times . . . the philosophical processes of our epoch . . . break(ing) with all the feelings that had been the possession of poetry and human thought] (28). As an example of this achievement, Reis cites what he believes to be Caeiro's most significant line of verse: "A Natureza é partes sem um todo" [Nature is parts without a whole] (28). Reis is not at all reluctant to comment on the "inevitable flaws" in Caeiro's poetry, which include the poet's use of the free-verse form; the "warm bath of Christian emotiveness" that pervades certain poems; and the love poetry written after O Guardador de Rebanhos, whose confused philosophy and "undisciplined" nature he blames on Caeiro's illness. But these flaws represent the challenge for Reis, who views Caeiro in Sebastian-like terms: "o Mestre, que primeiro, em vinte séculos de névoa, deixou ver os contornos dos montes, e a realidade directa das pedras e das flores" [the Master, the first in twenty centuries of fog to have allowed us to see the contours of the mountains and the direct reality of rocks and flowers] (33), and whose own verse takes up his cause.

4. In 1925, Pessoa introduced Caeiro posthumously to the Portuguese public by publishing verses from Caeiro's first and third collections in the literary review Athena. Although the earliest poems from O Guardador were penned in 1914, Pessoa dated the materials 1911–1912 to give the impression that Caeiro had written them a few years prior to his death in 1915. He similarly altered the dates of the Poemas Inconjuntos to 1913–1915, as if they were among the poet's last compositions.

5. Ruskin, "Pathetic Fallacy," 67–68.

6. Ibid., 68–69.

7. In its original form, the tenção consisted of a dialogue in verse between two or more troubadors, who would score points by rhyming the challenger's response. For example, here are the last two stanzas of a "tenção de maldizer" from the Cancioneiro da Biblioteca Nacional, in which two men are arguing about women:

—Joan Airas, vós perdestes o sen,
ca enas molheres sempr' ouve ben
e averá já, mais pera vós non.

—Joan Vaàsquiz, non dizedes ren,
ca todos se queixam delas por en
senon vós, que filhastes por en don. (Poesia e Prosa Medievais, 97)

[João Airas, you've lost your senses,
because there was always good in women
and there will always be, but not for you.

—João Vasquez, you don't say anything
because everyone here complains about them in that way
except for you, who was rewarded for your defense of them.]

8. For other comments about the differences between Caeiro and Whitman, see Hatherly, "Pessoa/Caeiro vs. Walt Whitman."

9. Verde, *Obra Completa*, 60.

Chapter 5: The Poetry of Ricardo Reis

1. For information on the cultural politics of such figures as Maurras and Hulme, see Sternhell, *The Birth of Fascist Ideology*.

2. Massaud Moisés, *Pequeno Dicionário*, 28–29. One wonders if Pessoa did not have Gonzaga in mind when he constructed his biography of Ricardo Reis—despite the fact that the Reis persona is Gonzaga's mirror opposite. A monarchist dissatisfied with the policies of Portuguese Republicanism, Reis exiled himself to the former Portuguese colony of Brazil.

Although born in Portugal in 1744, Gonzaga was the son of a Pernambucan diplomat and he spent most of his life in Brazil. He is best known for his volume *Marília de Dirceu*, which is a collection of love poems in the neoclassic tradition. A political activist, Gonzaga (along with fellow poet Claúdio Manuel da Costa) was accused of conspiring to overthrow the monarchy in Brazil—a plot which became known as the *Inconfidência Mineira*. Found guilty, he was jailed in Rio and deported to the Portuguese colony of Mozambique, where he lived a relatively active political and literary life until his death in 1810.

3. For more information on the Horatian character of Reis's odes, see Elia, "O Horaciano Reis."

4. Gonzaga, *Obras Completas*, 60.

5. Bocage, *Opera Omnia*, 2:128.

6. Ibid., 1:47.

7. See Pessoa, *Poemas Completos de Caeiro*, ed. Cunha, 2.

Chapter 6: The Poetry of Álvaro de Campos

1. Crespo, *A Vida Plural*, 321–22.

2. Pessoa, *Cartas de Amor*, 83.

3. With regard to their writing skills, Pessoa once remarked that "Campos [escreve] razoavelmente mas com lapsos . . . Reis melhor do que eu, mas com um purismo que considero exagerado" [Campos (writes) reasonably well but with lapses . . . Reis (writes) better than I, but with a purity that I consider exaggerated] (2:343).

4. Pessoa once stated that he was indebted to Freud for his observations on the relationship between tobacco smoke and onanism, or masturbation (2:299).

5. For further discussion of the affinities between Campos and his predecessors Whitman and Marinetti, consult Larsen and Sousa, "From Whitman." Regarding the homoerotic nature of Campos's poetry, see Lourenço, *Pessoa Revisitado*, especially 85–113. Pessoa's "own" homoerotic poems are "Epithalamium" and "Antinous." The former, written in 1913, is an ode about the fevered passion of the honeymoon night; the latter, appearing two years later, is more clearly homoerotic, retelling the tragic love story of the Roman emperor Hadrian and his servant boy

Antinous, who accidentally drowned in the Nile. Published in Lisbon, both of these poems are classical in theme and style, and neither has anything specific in common with Whitman. Writing to Simões in 1930, Pessoa declared that the English-language poems were his only "clearly obscene" works and that he had written them early in his career in order to "purge" himself of a "certain obsession" (2:290). For further discussion of these poems, see Vieira, *Sob o Ramo da Bétula*.

6. See, for example, Burg, *Sodomy and the Perception of Evil.*

7. One of the best close readings of "Tabacaria" is by Carlos Filipe Moisés, who regards the poem as central to the entire Pessoan corpus. For another study of the poem and its various translations into English, see Guyer, "Translating 'Tabacaria'."

8. Pessoa, *Poemas Completos de Caeiro,* ed. Cunha, 48.

Chapter 7: Text versus Work

1. Régio's essays, "Literatura Viva" and "Da Geração Modernista" [On the Modernist generation], appeared in the first and third issues of *Presença.* They were important in setting the agenda of the *presencistas,* whose literary and artistic interests ranged from European modernism to the cinema of Charlie Chaplin.

2. See *Presença,* 2:48.

3. This "Other" might be identified in terms of a split within the group in 1930. That year, Branquinho da Fonseca, Miguel Torga, and Edmundo de Bettencourt left *Presença* because they no longer agreed with its old-fashioned approach to "masters," "disciples," and literary schools. Casais Monteiro, who joined *Presença* in 1931 and who replaced Fonseca as literary director of the review, even denounced Torga as the "Inimigo de Deus e dos homens" [enemy of God and men]—the antithesis of Régio and the spiritual humanism that characterized the review (see Moisés, *Pequeno Dicionário,* 372–73).

4. Barthes, "From Work to Text," 164, 156–57.

5. Pessoa, *Poesias de Pessoa,* ed. Montalvor and Simões, 1:12–13.

6. Ultimately, the editors required three separate volumes for Pessoa's "unsuitable" works.

7. Pessoa, *Poesias de Pessoa,* ed. Montalvor and Simões, 1:15.

8. Of course, there is no question that style helps to distinguish the heteronyms from one another, and anyone familiar with Pessoa's writing in general could venture a good guess at which heteronym might have been responsible for a particular unsigned poem. There are many examples, however, where the interests of the heteronyms seem quite similar and where the stylistic boundaries between them seem to blur.

9. Ibid., 1:16–17.

10. Ibid., 3:12. See Berardinelli, "Remexendo," for comments on the problems in Montalvor and Simões's edition of Campos.

11. See their heated exchange in *Persona* 9 (1983):66–70. Also consult Jorge Nemésio's critique, *Os Inéditos de Fernando Pessoa e os Critérios do Dr. Gaspar Simões* [Fernando Pessoa's unpublished works and the criteria of Dr. Gaspar Simões].

12. Gallagher, *Portugal,* 91.

13. Stern, "The Ascension of Pessoa," 94.

14. Gallagher, *Portugal,* 93.

15. This was the theme of his essay entitled "Como Organizar Portugal" [How to organize Portugal], which appeared in 1919 in *Acção*—the official publication of the Núcleo de Acção Nacional, which nine years later published *O Interregno.* In terms of his economic philosophy, Pessoa has certain affinities with the Generation of 1870, whose members included the historian Oliveira Martins and the poet Antero de Quental. Unlike his predecessors, however, Pessoa was not drawn to socialism.

16. As Tom Gallagher has noted: "Around Rolão Preto . . . a cult of personality developed. The 'leader' toured the country on well publicized speaking campaigns and, according to one source, his movement, with a claimed 50,000 members, may have constituted a major political mobilization for Portugal . . . In August 1932 Rolão Preto was received by the British ambassador in Lisbon, and in July the following year the president himself even granted him an interview at the Belém palace" (*Portugal,* 90).

17. Ibid., 91.

18. In 1936, the government republished poems from *Mensagem* in honor of the tenth anniversary of the regime. This was a special publication which was prepared for the school system in the Portuguese colony of Macau. For more information on Portuguese writers and fascism, see Sousa, "Literature and Fascism."

19. Blanco, *Pessoa: Esboço de uma Bibliografia,* 20.

20. See the debate between Alfredo Margarido and Jacinto do Prado Coelho in *Colóquio,* as well as Sousa's discussion of their respective positions in "On Pessoa's Centrality."

21. See volume seven of *Persona* for a particularly virulent polemic between Honig and Witt August Willemsen over Honig's English translations.

22. In a statement on the Equipa Pessoa edition, Ivo Castro, who was appointed to lead the team, emphasized its mission: (1) to become familiarized with the archive; (2) to bring together the various documents relating to an individual text; (3) to order them chronologically and establish the origin of the text; (4) to determine the author's final point of intention with regard to the text and correct current editions; and (5) to publish the results in the form of critical-genetic editions and other archival supplements (see Castro, *Editar Pessoa,* 18.) For an update on the Equipa's work, see Rickard, "The Many in One."

23. See Cunha, "Da Impossibilidade."

24. Abelaira, "Qual Fernando Pessoa?" 10.

25. Barthes, "From Work to Text," 161.

Selected Bibliography

Editions of Pessoa's Works

Álvaro de Campos: Vida e Obras do Engenheiro. Ed. Teresa Rita Lopes. Lisbon: Estampa, 1990.

Cartas a Armando Cortes-Rodrigues. Lisbon: Livros Horizonte, 1985.

Cartas de Amor. Ed. David Mourão-Ferreira. Lisbon: Edições Ática, 1978.

O Guardador de Rebanhos. Facsimile. Ed. Ivo Castro. Lisbon: Publicações Dom Quixote, 1986.

Livro do Desassossego. 2 vols. Ed. Teresa Sobral Cunha. Lisbon: Editorial Presença, 1990–91.

Mensagem—Poemas Esotéricos. Critical edition. Ed. José Augusto Seabra. Spain: Archivos, 1993.

Obra Poética e em Prosa. 3 vols. Ed. António Quadros and Dalila Pereira da Costa. Oporto: Lello & Irmão Editores, 1986.

Poemas Completos de Alberto Caeiro. Ed. Teresa Sobral Cunha. Lisbon: Editorial Presença, 1994.

Poemas de Alberto Caeiro. Vol. 3. Ed. Luís de Montalvor and João Gaspar Simões. Lisbon, Edições Ática, 1946.

Poemas de Álvaro de Campos. Ed. Cleonice Berardinelli. Lisbon: Imprensa Nacional–Casa da Moeda, 1990.

Poesia de Fernando Pessoa. 2 vols. Ed. Adolfo Casais Monteiro. Lisbon: Editora Confluência, 1942.

Poesias de Fernando Pessoa. Vol. 1. Ed. Luís Montalvor and João Gaspar Simões. Lisbon: Edições Ática, 1942.

Quadras ao Gosto Popular. 2nd edition. Ed. Georg Rudolf Lind and Jacinto do Prado Coelho. Lisbon: Edições Ática, 1969.

Da República. Ed. Joel Serrão. Lisbon: Ática, 1978.

Translations

Always Astonished: Selected Prose. Trans. Edwin Honig. San Francisco: City Lights, 1988.

Antologia. Trans. Octavio Paz. Mexico City: Universidad Autónoma de México, 1962.

The Book of Disquietude. Trans. Richard Zenith. London: Carcanet, 1992.
Selected Poems. Trans. Edwin Honig. Chicago: Swallow Press, 1971.
Selected Poems. Trans. Peter Rickard. Edinburgh: Edinburgh University Press, 1971.

Other Sources

Abelaira, Augusto. "Qual Fernando Pessoa?" *Jornal de Letras, Artes e Ideias,* Aug. 24, 1993, 10.

Almeida, Onésimo Teotónio. *Mensagem: Uma Tentativa de Reinterpretação.* Angra do Heroísmo, Portugal: Direcção de Assuntos Culturais, 1987.

Antunes, Alfredo. *Saudade e Profetismo em Fernando Pessoa: Elementos para uma Antropologia Filosófica.* Braga, Portugal: Publicações da Faculdade de Filosofia, 1983.

Barthes, Roland. "The Death of the Author." In his *Image-Music-Text,* trans. Stephen Heath. New York: Hill and Wang, 1977.

———. "From Work to Text." In *Image-Music-Text.*

Berardinelli, Cleonice. *Poesia e Poética de Fernando Pessoa.* Rio de Janeiro, 1958.

———. "Remexendo no Espólio Pessoano." In *Actas: IV Congresso Internacional de Estudos Pessoanos* (Secção Brasileira). Vol. 1. Oporto, Portugal: Fundação Eng. António de Almeida, [1991].

Berardinelli, Cleonice, and Ivo Castro. *Defesa da Edição Crítica de Fernando Pessoa.* Lisbon, 1993.

Blanco, José, ed. *Fernando Pessoa: Esboço de uma Bibliografia.* Lisbon: Imprensa Nacional–Casa da Moeda, 1983.

Bloom, Harold. *The Anxiety of Influence: A Theory of Poetry.* New York: Oxford University Press, 1973.

———. "Borges, Neruda, and Pessoa: Hispanic-Portuguese Whitman." In his *The Western Canon: The Books and School of the Ages.* New York: Harcourt Brace, 1994.

Bocage, Manuel Maria Barbosa du. *Opera Omnia.* 6 vols. Ed. Hernâni Cidade. Lisbon: Livraria Bertrand, 1969–73.

Brooks, Mary Elizabeth. *A King for Portugal: The Madrigal Conspiracy, 1594–95.* Madison: University of Wisconsin Press, 1964.

Brown, Susan Margaret. "The Poetics of Fernando Pessoa's 'Drama em Gente': The Function of Alberto Caeiro and the Role of Walt Whitman." Ph.D. diss., University of North Carolina, 1987.

Burg, B. R. *Sodomy and the Perception of Evil: English Rovers in the Seventeenth Century.* New York: New York University Press, 1983.

Bürger, Peter. *Theory of the Avant-Garde.* Trans. Michael Shaw. Minneapolis: University of Minnesota Press, 1989.

Cabral, Manuel Villaverde. "The Aesthetics of Nationalism: Modernism and Authoritarianism in Early-Twentieth-Century Portugal." *Luso-Brazilian Review* 26, no. 1 (1989): 15–43.

Camões, Luís Vaz de. *Obras Completas*. 4th edition, 2 vols. Ed. Hernâni Cidade. Lisbon: Livraria Sá da Costa Editora, 1971.

Cancioneiro Geral de Garcia de Resende. 2 vols. Coimbra: Centro de Estudos Românicos, 1973.

Carvalho, Mário. "Tanto Pessoa Já Enjoa." *Jornal de Letras*, July 23, 1985.

Castro, Ivo. *Editar Pessoa*. Lisbon: Imprensa Nacional–Casa da Moeda, 1990.

Cláudio, Mário. Interview. "Nobre Maior que Pessoa." *Jornal de Letras*, Apr. 28, 1992, 9.

Coelho, Eduardo Prado, and Pierre Léglise-Costa. "O Amor e o Ressentimento." *Jornal de Letras*, Jan. 28, 1992, 10.

Coelho, Jacinto do Prado, ed. *Dicionário de Literatura*. 4 vols. Oporto: Figueirinhas, 1983.

———. *Diversidade e Unidade em Fernando Pessoa*. 2nd edition. Lisbon: Editorial Verbo, 1973.

———. "Sobre as Posições Políticas de Fernando Pessoa." *Colóquio* 23 (1975): 68.

Collins, Jim. *Uncommon Cultures: Popular Culture and Post-Modernism*. New York: Routledge, 1989.

Costa, Dalila L. Pereira da. *O Esoterismo de Fernando Pessoa*. Oporto: Lello & Irmão Editores, 1971.

Crespo, Ángel. *A Vida Plural de Fernando Pessoa*. Lisbon: Bertrand Editora, 1990.

Cunha, Teresa Sobral. "Ainda o *Livro do Desassossego*." *Colóquio* 129–30 (1993): 217–20.

———. Uma Edição, um Prefácio, um Tradutor." *Jornal de Letras*, Mar. 17, 1992, 12–13.

———. "Fernando Pessoa: Diário (Inédito) de 1906." *Colóquio* 95 (1987): 80–95.

———. "Da Impossibilidade de um *Texto Definitivo*." *Jornal de Letras*, Nov. 16, 1993, 16–17.

Duarte, Luís Fagundes. "Em Resposta a uma Crítica que o Não é." *Jornal de Letras*, July 27, 1993, 12–13.

Elia, Silvio. "O Horaciano Ricardo Reis." In *Actas: IV Congresso Internacional de Estudos Pessoanos*. Vol. 2. Oporto, Portugal: Fundação Eng. António de Almeida, [1991].

Eliot, T. S. "Tradition and the Individual Talent." In his *Selected Prose*, ed. John Hayward. Middlesex: Penguin, 1963.

Fotobibliografia de Fernando Pessoa: 1902–1935. Ed. João Rui de Sousa. Lisbon: Imprensa Nacional–Casa da Moeda, 1988.

Foucault, Michel. "What Is an Author?" In *Textual Strategies: Perspectives in Post-Structural Criticism*, ed. Josué V. Harari. Ithaca: Cornell University Press, 1979. 141–60.

Galhoz, Maria Aliete. "Em Torno ao Poema de Fernando Pessoa 'Ó Sino da Minha Aldeia'." In *Estudos Portugueses: Homenagem a Luciana Stegnano Picchio*. Lisbon: Difel, 1991. 743–57.

Gallagher, Tom. *Portugal: A Twentieth-Century Interpretation*. Manchester: Manchester University Press, 1983.

Gil, Augusto. *Versos*. 6th ed. Lisbon: Portugália, 1956.

Gonzaga, Tomás Antônio. *Obras Completas de Tomás Antônio Gonzaga: Poesias e Cartas Chilenas*. Ed. M. Rodrigues Lapa. Rio de Janeiro: Instituto Nacional do Livro, 1957.

Guyer, Leland. "Translating 'Tabacaria'." *Indiana Journal of Hispanic Literatures* 9 (1996): 187–209.

Hatherly, Ana. "Pessoa/Caeiro vs. Walt Whitman: A Destruição do Mestre." *Persona* 6 (1981): 7–19.

Jakobson, Roman, and Luciana Stegnano Picchio. "Les Oxymores Dialectiques de Fernando Pessoa." *Langages* 12 (1968): 9–27.

Jennings, H. D. *Os Dois Exílios: Fernando Pessoa na África do Sul*. Oporto: Centro de Estudos Pessoanos, 1984.

Joyce, James. *A Portrait of the Artist as a Young Man*. 6th ed. New York: Viking Press, 1966.

Júdice, Nuno. *A Era do "Orpheu."* Lisbon: Teorema, 1986.

———. "O Futurismo em Portugal." *Portugal Futurista*. vii–xiii.

Kristeva, Julia. *Desire in Language: A Semiotic Approach to Literature and Art*. Ed. Leon S. Roudiez. Trans. Thomas Gora, Alice Jardine, and Leon S. Roudiez. New York: Columbia University Press, 1984.

Larsen, Neil, and Ronald W. Sousa. "From Whitman (to Marinetti) to Álvaro de Campos: A Case Study in Materialist Approaches to Literary Influences. *Ideologies and Literature* 17 (1983): 94–115.

Lind, Georg Rudolf. *Estudos sobre Fernando Pessoa*. 4th ed. Lisbon: Imprensa Nacional–Casa da Moeda, 1981.

Lisboa, Eugénio. "Perfeição, Imperfeição." *Jornal de Letras*, Mar. 24, 1992, 7.

Lopes, Teresa Rita. "A Crítica da Edição Crítica." *Colóquio* 125–26 (1992): 199–218.

———. "Pessoa Normalizado para a CEE." *Jornal de Letras*, Jan. 21, 1992, 15–17.

———. "Pessoa Normalizado para a CEE: Segundo Capítulo." *Jornal de Letras*, Feb. 4, 1992, 20–21.

———, ed. *Pessoa por Conhecer*. 2 vols. Lisbon: Editorial Estampa, 1990.

Lourenço, Eduardo. *Fernando Pessoa Revisitado: Leitura Estruturante do Drama em Gente*. Oporto: Inova, 1981.

Macedo, Helder. "Inquérito: Fernando Pessoa Hoje." *Colóquio* 88 (1985): 133–34.

———. "A *Mensagem* e as Mensagens de Oliveira Martins e de Junqueiro." *Colóquio* 103 (1988): 28–39.

Margarido, Alfredo. "Sobre as Posições Políticas de Fernando Pessoa." *Colóquio* 23 (1975): 66–68.

Marques, Oswaldino. "Fingimento em Cadeia—ou o Abismo Revisitado: A Respeito de um Poema de Fernando Pessoa." *Minas Gerais Suplemento Literário*, Dec. 24, 1990, 2–5.

McGuirk, Bernard, ed. *Three Persons on One: A Centenary Tribute to Fernando Pessoa*. University of Nottingham: Monographs in the Humanities 5, 1988.

Meireles, Cecília, ed. *Novos Poetas de Portugal*. Rio de Janeiro: Edições Dois Mundos, 1944.

Moisés, Carlos Filipe. *O Poema e as Máscaras*. Coimbra: Livraria Almedina, 1981.

Moisés, Leyla Perrone. "A *Minha* Experiência do Catálogo da Europália." *Jornal de Letras,* Feb. 18, 1992, 31.

Moisés, Massaud, ed. *Pequeno Dicionário de Literatura Portuguesa*. São Paulo: Editora Cultrix, 1981.

Monteiro, Adolfo Casais. *A Poesia de Fernando Pessoa*. Lisbon: Imprensa Nacional–Casa da Moeda, 1985.

Monteiro, George, ed. *The Man Who Never Was*. Providence: Gávea-Brown, 1982.

———. "Poe/Pessoa." *Comparative Literature* 40 (1988): 134–49.

———. "The Song of the Reaper: Pessoa and Wordsworth." *Portuguese Studies* 5 (1989): 71–80.

Nemésio, Jorge. *Os Inéditos de Fernando Pessoa e os Critérios do Dr. Gaspar Simões*. Lisbon: Editora Eros, 1957.

Nobre, António. *Só*. 10th ed. Oporto: Livraria Tavares Martins, 1955.

Nunes, Maria Arminda Zaluar. *O Cancioneiro Popular em Portugal*. Lisbon: Instituto de Cultura Portuguesa, 1978.

Pascoaes, Teixeira de. *A Saudade e o Saudosismo*. Lisbon: Assírio & Alvim, 1988.

Perloff, Marjorie. *The Futurist Moment: Avant-Garde, Avant Guerre, and the Language of Rupture*. Chicago: University of Chicago Press, 1986.

Poesia e Prosa Medievais. Ed. Maria Ema Tarracha Ferreira. Lisbon: Editora Ulisséia, n.d.

Portugal Futurista. 2nd facsimile edition. Lisbon: Contexto Editora, 1982.

Presença. Facsimile edition. 2 vols. Lisbon: Contexto, 1993.

Quadros, António. *Fernando Pessoa: Vida, Personalidade e Génio*. 4th ed. Lisbon: Publicações Dom Quixote, 1992.

Rickard, Peter. "Fernando Pessoa." In Fernando Pessoa, *Selected Poems,* trans. Peter Rickard. Edinburgh: Edinburgh University Press, 1971, 1–61.

———. "The Many in One." *Times Literary Supplement,* Oct. 17, 1997, 27.

Rocha, Andrée Crabbé. *Garcia de Resende e o "Cancioneiro Geral."* Lisbon: Livraria Bertrand, 1979.

Roditi, Edouard. "The Several Names of Fernando Pessoa." *Poetry* 87 (1955): 26–29.

Ruskin, John. "Of the Pathetic Fallacy." *The Genius of John Ruskin*. Ed. John D. Rosenberg. New York: George Braziller, 1963. 61–71.

Sá-Carneiro, Mário de. *Cartas a Fernando Pessoa*. 2 vols. Lisbon: Edições Ática, 1959.

Sacramento, Mário. *Fernando Pessoa: Poeta da Hora Absurda*. Lisbon: Contraponto, 1958.

Santos, Maria Irene Ramalho de Sousa. "Atlantic Poets: Discovery as Metaphor and Ideology." In *The Continuing Presence of Walt Whitman: The Life after the Life,* ed. Robert K. Martin. Iowa City: University of Iowa Press, 1992. 152–66.

———. "Poetas e Pássaros: Sobre a Consciência Poética em Pessoa e Stevens." *Colóquio* 88 (1985): 94–101.

Saraiva, Mário. *O Caso Clínico de Fernando Pessoa.* Lisbon: Editora Referendo, 1990.

Seabra, José Augusto. *Fernando Pessoa ou o Poetodrama.* Lisbon: Imprensa Nacional–Casa da Moeda, 1988.

———. *O Heterotexto Pessoano.* Lisbon: Dinalivro, 1985.

Sena, Jorge de. *Fernando Pessoa & Ca. Heterónima: Estudos Coligidos 1940–1978.* 2nd ed. Lisbon: Edições 70, 1984.

Serrão, Joel. "Da República Portuguesa e de Fernando Pessoa nela." In *Da República.* 7–98.

———. *Do Sebastianismo ao Socialismo.* Lisbon: Livros Horizonte, 1983.

Severino, Alexandrino E. *Fernando Pessoa na África do Sul: A Formação Inglesa de Fernando Pessoa.* Lisbon: Publicações Dom Quixote, 1983.

Silveira, Pedro da. "Fernando Pessoa: A sua Estreia aos 14 Anos e Outras Poesias de 1902 a 1905." *Revista da Biblioteca Nacional* 3, no. 2 (1988): 97–121.

Simões, João Gaspar. *Vida e Obra de Fernando Pessoa: História duma Geração.* 5th ed. Lisbon: Publicações Dom Quixote, 1987.

Sousa, Ronald W. "Literature and Portuguese Fascism: The Face of the Salazarist State, Preceded by Two Pre-Faces." In *Fascismo y Experiencia Literaria: Reflexiones para una Recanonización,* ed. Hernán Vidal. Minneapolis: Institute for the Study of Ideologies and Literature, 1985.

———. "On Pessoa's Continued Centrality in Portuguese Culture." *Ideologies and Literature* 3, no. 2 (1988): 39–50.

———. "Pessoa the Messenger." In his *The Rediscoverers: Major Writers in the Portuguese Literature of National Regeneration.* University Park: Pennsylvania State University Press, 1981. 130–60.

Stern, Irwin. "The Ascension of Fernando Pessoa." *Lusitânia* 1, no. 3 (1990): 93–96.

Sternhell, Zeev, with Mario Sznajder and Maia Asheri. *The Birth of Fascist Ideology: From Cultural Revolution to Political Revolution.* Trans. David Maisel. Princeton: Princeton University Press, 1994.

Suárez, José I. "Portugal's *Saudosismo* Movement: An Esthetics of Sebastianism." *Luso-Brazilian Review* 28, no. 1 (1991): 129–40.

L'Univers Pessoa. Brussels: Centre Culturel de la Communante Française, 1991.

Verde, Cesário. *Obra Completa.* 3rd ed. Ed. Joel Serrão. Lisbon: Portugália, n.d.

Vieira, Yara Frateschi. *Sob o Ramo da Bétula: Fernando Pessoa e o Erotismo Vitoriano.* Campinas: Editora da Unicamp, 1989.

Wheeler, Douglas. *Republican Portugal: A Political History 1910–1926.* Madison: University of Wisconsin Press, 1978.

Zenith, Richard. "Uma Desassossegada Investigadora." *Jornal de Letras,* Mar. 24, 1992, 6.

———. "Um Novo 'Livro do Desassossego'." *Colóquio* 125–26 (1992): 219–22.

Index